Microsoft SharePoint for Business Executives: Q&A Handbook

100 Essential Questions and Answers about SharePoint 2010 for Executives considering SharePoint deployments

Peter Ward

Pavlo Andrushkiw

Paul Galvin

Richard Harbridge

Michael Hinckley

William Nagle

[PACKT] enterprise
PUBLISHING   professional expertise distilled

BIRMINGHAM - MUMBAI

Microsoft SharePoint for Business Executives: Q&A Handbook

First published: May 2012

Production Reference: 1170512

Published by Packt Publishing Ltd.
Livery Place
35 Livery Street
Birmingham B3 2PB, UK.

ISBN 978-1-84968-610-5

www.packtpub.com

Cover Image by Darryl Nitke (darrylnitke@hotmail.com)

Credits

Authors

Peter Ward

Pavlo Andrushkiw

Paul Galvin

Richard Harbridge

Michael Hinckley

William Nagle

Reviewers

Keith A Barros

L Scot Bobo

Jeffrey L. Bromberger

Yaroslav Pentsarskyy

Muhammad A. Piracha

Acquisition Editor

Stephanie Moss

Lead Technical Editors

Shreerang Deshpande

Chris Rodrigues

Technical Editors

Joyslita D'Souza

Veronica Fernandes

Project Coordinators

Kushal Bhardwaj

Sai Gamare

Proofreader

Chris Smith

Indexer

Tejal Daruwale

Graphics

Manu Joseph

Production Coordinator

Aparna Bhagat

Cover Work

Aparna Bhagat

Foreword

There are many approaches to starting a SharePoint project.

In my experience all the big ones start with a team of people presenting this bright perfect future with them leading us. They are going to solve all your existing issues and then hold your hand into the future. You listen closely to the advice of the team and the supporting propaganda from Microsoft, assemble a team across all departments, present to the CFO, the Chairman, and Department heads.

The ideas come pouring out. Every department's idea starts with "I want to be able to...It would be great if...". You think you hit pay dirt, your end users are going to help you build a roadmap based on true knowledge and all they need is your guidance based feedback.

At some point you may arrive at the conclusion that SharePoint is the platform to take you into the future.

Then you learn that a great deal of people have assumptions disguised as basic understanding and you don't know where to start. So, many of your great ideas become obstacles because you are spending the time explaining what you thought was basic knowledge to many and you only realize the impact of some of your decisions at the no-turning-back point. The simple definition of the Cloud is enough to push your limits, combine that again with the realization that many of your end users had created their own way of doing things, and those things are not always in line with or have anything to do with the job they are supposed to be doing.

So when I began to read the questions and answers of this book, I began to develop a completely new paradigm of how to manage, appreciate, and create business value with the SharePoint technology.

As a CIO managing multiple technologies grappling with business requests, and return on investment justification of my decisions, this book does a great job spelling out the pitfalls and providing a map for success. It reminds us to ask the basic questions and then takes the authors' experiences to guide you through the answers.

At times the authors' observations and advice are thought-provoking and hit home for Information Technology (IT) leaders and make them think about future SharePoint projects and how they should be done, which is the idea behind the book. You sometimes just need someone to spell it out, remind you to not assume and just ask the people in the room a simple question before things go too far.

Once someone's assumptions have been replaced with fact, you have a direction to move forward, and people who were once just involved in your project become excited to be a part of the team. This book is a simple reminder that taking the time to ask questions and spell things out makes all the difference to your success.

From experience, SharePoint is a powerful platform, which can be most challenging if not looked at with the proper insights and thought leadership. The more powerful the platform the more ways it can pull you from the original roadmap that you intended to follow. After reading this book, the main observation I had was that it has a great deal of advice to any executive who is a manager of the SharePoint technology and wishes to provide leadership as well—the kind of leadership that has to do with enabling others to fulfill their full potential better.

Peter Grazioli,
former VP/CIO, Young Broadcasting

About the Authors

Peter Ward has worked with Collaboration Technology for over 20 years and is the founder of Soho Dragon Solutions, a New York-based SharePoint consultancy. He has worked with some of the largest and most profitable companies in the U.S. and also the small ones, which he calls the Fortune 5,000,000.

He has always been a software guy, but is not much of a gadgeteer. In fact, he's probably a late adopter. He teaches yoga part time in NYC. He likes to serve up the perfect vegetarian dish. He has co-authored *Microsoft SharePoint 2010 End User Guide: Business Performance Enhancement* and *Workflow in SharePoint 2010: Real World Business Workflow Solutions*.

I would like to thank my wife Peggy for being the unofficial editor of the book, even though she uses Lotus Notes at work and her company is the most anti-Microsoft company out there.

I would also like to thank the following people who assisted me with reviews and valuable input: Steve Malcolm, Ron Margalit, Jeff Gellman, Chris Geier, Jim Mc Fadden, Kanwal Khipple, and Michael Albers.

Pavlo Andrushkiw, MCSE, MCTS, and CTT+, has spent nearly a decade in the Microsoft space, delivering complex infrastructure solutions to a plethora of clients in various verticals. In his IT career, he has already been a Network Engineer, Systems Administrator, Web Developer/Administrator, Consultant, Trainer, Project Manager, and Infrastructure Architect. His passion and enthusiasm for properly integrating Microsoft stack products has made its way into the Amazon EC2 cloud, where he now migrates and deploys complex production environments for enterprise clients.

> A special thanks to God through Whom all things are possible, to my parents for their encouragement in all my endeavors, to my beautiful wife who is pregnant with our first child and is still managing to provide unrelenting patience and support, and to my future child who is already grumbling about Microsoft licensing practices from the womb.

Paul Galvin has been working in the IT industry since 1991. He started as a staff programmer and began consulting in 1994 and never stopped. In 2008 he was awarded an MVP and in 2010 he was acknowledged to be in a group of the 50 most influential people within the SharePoint business community.

Richard Harbridge is an internationally recognized expert in Microsoft SharePoint. He has defined, architected, developed, and implemented well over a hundred SharePoint solutions from small implementations on a single server to implementations with over 80,000 users in international organizations.

He is a contributing author for the business side of NothingButSharePoint.com and is also an active facilitator for the SharePoint Business Community to enable people, groups, and organizations to work more effectively to collaborate and achieve a greater level of shared understanding around non-technical SharePoint-related challenges.

Michael Hinckley MCITP, MCTS, has been specializing in solution architecture for organizations that span from small businesses to global corporations for over 10 years. He is a recognized speaker and evangelist for Microsoft SharePoint and Business Intelligence stacks. His driving goal is to deliver successful and efficient business solutions for clients.

William Nagle is the Director of Field Operations at K2, where he helps organizations and partners realize the business value of process automation around SharePoint and other Microsoft technologies. He joined K2 after eight years of service at Microsoft Corporation where his career spanned the E-Business Server product groups including Commerce Server and BizTalk. His interest shifted towards helping companies efficiently manage business processes while working as a Senior Consultant at Microsoft Consulting Services.

About the Reviewers

Keith A Barros has over 20 years of IT management experience. He has managed at all levels in consulting, manufacturing, retail, financial, and education industries. Strategic and collaborative technologies coupled with process and organizational change are his specialties.

He has been an adjunct professor teaching graduate and undergraduate classes in technology. He has a B.S. in Management Science from Kean University and an M.B.A. in Marketing from Seton Hall University.

L Scot Bobo has been an Internal Technology professional since 1997. During that time, he's been involved with projects related to Exchange, SharePoint, IIS, and HelpDesk Resolution. He began his career as an Implementation Consultant and went on to become a Project Manager, Group Manager, and is now the Internal Systems Manager for a Microsoft Gold partner.

He has also collaborated on the book, *Microsoft SharePoint 2010 End User Guide: Business Performance Enhancement* written by Peter Ward and Mike McCabe.

I would like to thank Peter Ward for giving me the opportunity to be involved with this book. I would also like to thank my family, for giving me the opportunity to spend late, quiet nights working on it.

Jeffrey L. Bromberger has been an IT professional in the Finance Industry for the better part of the last 20 years. He specializes in IT Service Management, Call Center administration, and KPI reporting. He regularly writes detailed technical reports for various auditing entities, both internal and external to his firm. He is trained as a molecular biologist and being a Unix administrator at heart he takes almost everything he reads with a grain of salt, especially Microsoft documents.

Yaroslav Pentsarskyy has been involved in SharePoint solution architecture and implementation since 2003. As a Microsoft MVP since 2009 he keeps in close touch with the SharePoint product team. He frequently presents at local and worldwide tech events as well as online; you can always find a fresh bit of SharePoint information on his blog `sharemuch.com`. He is also the author of a few SharePoint titles: *Top 60 custom solutions built on SharePoint 2010*, *SharePoint 2010 branding in practice*, and *Microsoft SharePoint 2010 and Windows PowerShell 2.0: Expert Cookbook*.

Muhammad A. Piracha is a Senior Software Engineer at Bamboo Solutions Corporation. Based in Reston, Virginia, Bamboo Solutions is a leading provider of software solutions for the Microsoft SharePoint platform. He has over 15 years of experience in building document management software applications using various Microsoft products. He has experience in a variety of capacities, including architecting, designing, and developing software for SharePoint technologies since its 2003 release. When he is not on a computer writing code, he enjoys the time spent with his family and outdoor activities.

www.PacktPub.com

Support files, eBooks, discount offers, and more

You might want to visit www.PacktPub.com for support files and downloads related to your book.

Did you know that Packt offers eBook versions of every book published, with PDF and ePub files available? You can upgrade to the eBook version at www.PacktPub.com and, as a print book customer, you are entitled to a discount on the eBook copy. Get in touch with us at service@packtpub.com for more details.

At www.PacktPub.com, you can also read a collection of free technical articles, sign up for a range of free newsletters, and receive exclusive discounts and offers on Packt books and eBooks.

http://PacktLib.PacktPub.com

Do you need instant solutions to your IT questions? PacktLib is Packt's online digital book library. Here, you can access, read, and search across Packt's entire library of books.

Why Subscribe?

- Fully searchable across every book published by Packt
- Copy and paste, print and bookmark content
- On demand and accessible via web browser

Free Access for Packt account holders

If you have an account with Packt at www.PacktPub.com, you can use this to access PacktLib today and view nine entirely free books. Simply use your login credentials for immediate access.

Instant Updates on New Packt Books

Get notified! Find out when new books are published by following @PacktEnterprise on Twitter, or the *Packt Enterprise* Facebook page.

Table of Contents

Preface   **1**

Chapter 1: Defining a SharePoint IT Strategy   **11**

  Q: Can you define what a strategy is?   **11**

  Q: What is an IT strategy?   **12**

  Q: How do you create a SharePoint IT strategy?   **15**

    Day 1: Diagnostics   15

      Intro to workshop—discussion   15

      Company background—discussion   15

      The Focus on IT environment—discussion   16

      Current IT core applications—discussion   16

      Future IT core applications—discussion   16

      Review—discussion   17

    Day 2: The treatment plan   17

      Initial findings and review—discussion   17

      The Gap analysis   17

      Priorities, actions, and agreement   17

      Review—discussion   18

    Day 3: A successful SharePoint implementation plan   19

      Next steps—discussion   19

      Summary and close out   19

  Q: What is the intended outcome of the workshop?   **20**

  Q: Who needs to be involved with the process?   **22**

  Funny you should say that...   **23**

    Q: Do I need to get the CEO involved?   23

    Q: Why is a SharePoint strategy different than other IT products?   23

    Q: What are the pitfalls of a SharePoint strategy?   25

    Q: Why do we really need an IT strategy?   26

  Digging deeper   **27**

    Q: Any final words of advice on this?   27

  Summary   **28**

Chapter 2: Just Enough Governance   29

Q. What is governance?   30

Q. Why do we need it?   30

Q: So where do I start with governance?   30

Q: Who should be involved with SharePoint governance?   33

Case study: Include everyone   34

Q: Is it worth hiring a consulting firm to create your company's governance documentation?   35

Q: Why does it seem that SharePoint requires more governance than other technologies?   36

Funny you should say that...   38

Q: How do you define "just enough governance"?   38

Q: How do I strike this so-called "balance"?   38

Q: Well, we have got this far without governance with SharePoint, so why bother?   39

Q: Our existing governance plan hasn't improved deployments or reduced frustrations; any suggestions?   40

Q: Won't governance slow down the speed of innovation?   41

Digging deeper   41

Q: Where can I find further information on a governance approach with SharePoint?   42

Summary   42

Chapter 3: Deployment Roadmap   43

Q: Which edition of SharePoint is right for me?   44

SharePoint Foundation   44

SharePoint Server 2010 Standard   45

SharePoint Server 2010 Enterprise   45

FAST Search Server 2010 for SharePoint 2010   45

SharePoint Server 2010 for Internet Sites, Standard   46

SharePoint Server 2010 for Internet Sites, Enterprise   47

Microsoft Office 365   47

FAST Search Server 2010 for Internet Sites   47

Q: Where should I deploy SharePoint? What choices do I really have?   47

On-premise   48

Hosted   49

Cloud   51

Hybrid   52

So what do I choose?   52

Q: What about licensing? What are my options and how much will it cost?   53

What edition of SharePoint does my company need?   53

Who are my end users? 54
How many servers will run SharePoint? 55
How many people or devices will access SharePoint? 55
Is my company licensed for the Microsoft products that are needed to
run SharePoint? 56
Enterprise Agreement 56
Q: SharePoint 2010 Development, Quality Assurance,
Production—how many farms do I actually need? **57**
Q: What do I need to know about storage requirements and their
impact on my deployment strategy? **59**
Estimating content database storage 60
Data scale 61
Q: Intranet, extranet—which SharePoint topology is right for me? **61**
Intranets 62
Extranets 62
Public-facing Internet sites 63
Q: What about authentication for end users; what options are
available to me? **63**
Funny you should say that... **64**
Q: Is there any way for me to migrate my existing licenses, instead of
having to obtain new ones? 64
Q: What do I need to know about web browsers, tablets, and mobile
phones? 65
Web browsers 65
Mobile phones 66
Tablets 66
Q: Why are companies resistant to My Sites; can this attitude ever
change? 66
Q: I've heard that Office 2010 is the only version that integrates with
SharePoint 2010. Is this true, and what are some other MS products
that integrate with SharePoint 2010? 67
Disaster recovery 67
Antivirus 68
Security 68
Monitoring and management 68
Project management 68
Business intelligence 68
Client applications 69
Digging deeper **69**
SharePoint editions 69
SharePoint licensing 69
Capacity planning 70
Extranet topologies 70

Public-facing SharePoint sites	70
Authentication mechanisms	70
Summary	**71**
Chapter 4: SharePoint in the Clouds	**73**
Q: What options do I actually have for cloud-based SharePoint 2010?	**74**
Public cloud	75
Private cloud	76
Community cloud	77
Hybrid cloud	77
Q: How can I use Amazon Web Services for SharePoint 2010?	**78**
Amazon Elastic Compute Cloud	79
Amazon Elastic Block Store	79
Amazon Virtual Private Cloud	80
Elastic Load Balancing	80
Q: This doesn't sound like a turn-key solution. Where does Amazon's responsibility end and where does mine begin?	**81**
Amazon infrastructure	82
Windows infrastructure	83
SharePoint infrastructure	83
Q: Can I create a Microsoft private cloud solution for SharePoint?	**84**
Technology Stack	84
Licensing	85
Benefits	85
Q: Office 365 and SharePoint Online—how many offerings and plans are actually out there?	**85**
Dedicated versus Standard	86
Small businesses	86
Midsize businesses and enterprises	87
Education	87
Kiosk Plans	87
Q: What authentication options do I have for SharePoint Online?	**88**
Microsoft Online Services IDs	88
Microsoft Windows Live IDs	88
ADFS 2.0 and SSO	89
Q: What about Windows Azure and SharePoint 2010? How can I take advantage of this offering?	**89**
Service	90
Data	90

Funny you should say that...   **90**
  Q: Security is always a concern. What can I do to secure my SharePoint
  deployment in the cloud?   91
    Amazon security   91
    SharePoint security   91
  Q: How do I migrate my on-premise deployment to SharePoint Online?
  What are my options?   92
  Q: I've been told that SharePoint online has less features than its
  on-premise counterpart. What is it missing?   94
Digging deeper   **95**
  Amazon Web Services   95
  Private Clouds   95
  Office 365   95
    Migration   96
  Windows Azure   96
Summary   **96**

Chapter 5: SharePoint and Important Trends   **99**
Q: How big is SharePoint to Microsoft?   **100**
Q: Which IT trends matter?   **100**
  Q: What are the user experience trends?   102
    Users choose their interface and the sources for those interfaces   103
    Users choose between desktop, web, mobile, and other forms of technology-driven
    information consumption   103
    Mobile, tablet, and other forms of consumption have had mixed experiences   104
    One browser doesn't rule them all   104
    Growing screen resolutions and growing accessibility expectations   105
  Q: What are the IT delivery trends?   105
  Q: What are the collaboration and communication trends?   106
    Q: Do social computing technologies really help businesses, and is SharePoint really
    a social computing platform?   108
  Q: What are the data and information trends and how is SharePoint
  meeting this demand?   110
    What is BI for the masses?   111
    The Microsoft BI Stack   112
    Search first, ask questions later   113
    SharePoint and FAST   115
Funny you should say that...   **116**
  Q: What are the security trends?   116
    SharePoint permission sprawl   116
    Environment security   117
  Q: How agile is SharePoint?   117
    What is agile?   117

Q: SharePoint applications: Is it better to buy or build?   119
    Q: What are the reasons for the rapid growth of more SharePoint applications
that you can download and activate?   120
Digging deeper   **121**
  Q: What are your internal corporate trends?   122
  Q: What are the consumer trends?   122
  Q: What are other industry and technology trends?   123
Summary   **124**
Chapter 6: How to get the .NET Developers on Board Quickly?   **127**
**Q: What's so different about SharePoint development compared to
.NET development?**   **128**
Q: How should we approach SharePoint development?   **132**
  Have a source-control strategy   132
  Create a development environment   133
  Build a User Acceptance Testing (UAT) environment   134
  Build a production environment   135
  Deployment strategy   135
Q: What roadblocks do new SharePoint developers face?   **136**
  Complementary SharePoint technology   137
  Q: How do we avoid mistakes in the early stages?   139
  Q: Can you provide an example of when a straight .NET development
is more appropriate than SharePoint .NET?   140
Q: What do I need to know to get started in SharePoint development?   **141**
  .NET development   141
  How SharePoint features function within the platform   141
  How to deploy customizations   141
  Q: What technical environment do I need to get started with SharePoint
development?   142
Q: Do developers ever resist the SharePoint developer route?   **143**
  SharePoint development is not considered professional development   143
  Developers do not want to work within a product   144
  Most developers do not want to be end user focused   144
Funny you should say that...   **144**
  Q: How do I know that my developers just do not have the SharePoint
knowledge?   144
  Q: Does a SharePoint developer need better than normal
communication skills?   146
Digging deeper   **147**
  Q: How can I learn SharePoint development as fast as possible?   147
    Find a user group   148
    Connect through social media   148

Forums	149
Q: What SharePoint books do you recommend for learning development?	149
Summary	**150**

Chapter 7: Growing SharePoint Capacity and Meeting Staffing Resource Needs — 151

Q: What are the minimal SharePoint deployment and technical skill set I can get away with?	**151**
Q: What would be the typical SharePoint skill sets needed for different company sizes?	**153**
Q: How easy is it to train in-house technical staff on SharePoint?	**155**
Q: What kind of training resources are available?	**156**
Funny you should say that...	**158**
Q: Should I listen to recruiters on job descriptions?	159
SharePoint Developer:	159
Preferred requirements:	160
Q: What are the hidden costs of SharePoint?	161
Q: Is there a good approach when using SharePoint for a "charge back" model to the business?	162
Q: Is it worth purchasing a Microsoft Enterprise License Agreement?	163
Digging deeper	**164**
Q: How do I start to grow capacity?	165
Q: What if I can't get budget to grow capacity?	165
Q: How do I define if SharePoint has been a success after one year?	165
Summary	**167**

Chapter 8: Managing your First SharePoint Project — 169

Q: What factors should you take into consideration?	**170**
Team skill and experience	170
Size and scope of the project	170
Your customer	171
Configuration versus customization	171
Q: Why is a SharePoint first project different to other technologies' first project?	**172**
Case Study: The insurance firm	173
End-user community	174
Anti-patterns	174
Q: How do we decide upon our first project's scope?	**175**
Principles of good business scope	176
Technical scope	177
Sirens of Greek mythology	178
Technical skill set	179

Q: How do you plan for and design your first SharePoint project solution? **179**
  Planning 179
  Designing 181
Q: What's the best way to execute? **182**
  Work iteratively 182
  Share, share, share 183
Q: Should you implement in phases? **183**
Funny you should say that... **184**
  Q: How do you organize your SharePoint team? 184
  Q: How do you leverage success? 185
Digging deeper **186**
  Q: What problems should you anticipate with your first project? 186
    Q: Who should be the first business unit for a SharePoint deployment? 186
    Q. How easy is it to change from configuration to customization in a project? 187
Summary **187**

Chapter 9: Now What? **189**
Q: How do I apply the concepts from this book to produce results? **189**
Q: I have heard SharePoint projects often fail. How can this be avoided? **190**
Q: How do I choose a company to partner with? **191**
Q: Is it easy to offshore SharePoint development? **192**
Q: How do I estimate a SharePoint development project? **193**
Q: How easy is it for Java development teams to learn .NET SharePoint development? **195**
Funny you should say that... **195**
  Q: How do I write an RFP for a technology that I'm not familiar with? 195
    You get what you ask for 196
    People are fooled by price 196
    Time is money 197
    Beauty is in the eye of the beholder 197
Digging deeper **198**
  Q: Can a SharePoint deployment really help my career? 198
    Formulation 199
    Concentration 199
    Momentum 200
    Stability 200
    Breakthrough 200
    Mastery 201
    Other operating states 201
Summary **202**
Index **203**

Preface

The depth and breadth of the SharePoint technology can be quite daunting to any executive who is managing a SharePoint technical team, or is facing the challenge of determining the next steps with an upcoming SharePoint deployment within their organization.

This book is structured to answer those initial questions and provide you with a roadmap to understand the SharePoint technology, as well answering questions that you should be asking or will be asked by other departments' managers or an executive board.

This book will demystify the planning and managing of the SharePoint technology and you will learn how to identify and implement high business-value projects with simple, non-technical answers.

Why this book

All six authors have participated in successful SharePoint deployments within different industries and on various scales. All have witnessed train-wreck deployments that could have been avoided if, at an executive level, there was a better understanding of the application and a wider awareness of the business impact of the product, installation, and development options prior to project kick-off meetings or even determining the locations of servers.

Although some of these so called "train wreck" projects had highly technical and experienced professionals making what appeared to be logical decisions with an approach that had worked on previous non-SharePoint IT project deployments, most processes fell short because of a lack of understanding of the product deployment approaches, capabilities, technical skills required, and the reactions and responses to SharePoint deployments by the business community.

Microsoft may promote SharePoint as putting the business in the driving seat of IT, but the road to hell is paved with good intentions and could be avoided, if there was a better understanding of the journey ahead.

Going off the rails

Often businesses start off with an installation of the free SharePoint version with enthusiastic business sponsors who have visions of how SharePoint could meet their business needs. This is normally reinforced by reading the blazingly successful case studies from the Microsoft website, and by attending webinars/seminars provided by the Microsoft Partner community.

Then SharePoint goes viral. That is, employees who have used SharePoint in previous jobs start saying SharePoint can do this, that, and so on. (Note that they are *not* saying how it was done, and the budget and the resources that it needed.)

Fast forward three months—multiple site collections and team sites, an uninformed IT department, a stack of SharePoint books, and a lot of reactionary effort unrelated to people's jobs is spent on trying to learn a product and making it fit to a business process.

Fast forward another three months and you see disillusion among the user base, IT wondering how to get a handle on this technology, the support from users is waning, and the person who spearheaded the initial SharePoint activity over the past six months and who was leading the learning of the SharePoint technology has left and is working for someone else.

This train wreck story (yes, so early in the book) might seem a bit extreme, but it is not far from the truth, from what the authors have witnessed and is a classic case of not thinking ideas through.

William Deresiewicz, who gave a lecture to the plebe class at the United States Military Academy at West Point in October 2009 said:

> *I find for myself that my first thought is never my best thought. My first thought is always someone else's; it's always what I've already heard about the subject, always the conventional wisdom. It's only by concentrating, sticking to the question, being patient, letting all the parts of my mind come into play, that I arrive at an original idea. By giving my brain a chance to make associations, draw connections, take me by surprise. And often even that idea doesn't turn out to be very good. I need time to think about it, too, to make mistakes and recognize them, to make false starts and correct them, to outlast my impulses, to defeat my desire to declare the job done and move on to the next thing.*

The moment I hear someone say they are 'Trying to do something', it normally means that they will not succeed in the task. You don't try to cross the road, you cross the road.

How this book will save you money, and, just possibly, your career

With a section header like this, it sounds too good to be true. However, if a project is not staffed correctly, implemented without a business strategy, or is misaligned with the business's strategy, problems will arise. This may sound obvious, but a .NET developer cannot start working immediately with the API without training or coaching and a .NET developer who may have technical knowledge, is not an administrator. This knowledge and insight can be key to a successful SharePoint deployment.

This is a very common mistake made by companies, including Microsoft Partners, attempting to build a SharePoint practice. This is covered in more detail in *Chapter 6, How to get the .NET Developers on Board Quickly?*, and *Chapter 8, Managing your First SharePoint Project*, of this book.

This book follows the **Data, Information, Knowledge, and Wisdom (DIKW)** hierarchy, where the authors have applied their wisdom to knowledge of the SharePoint technology and projects that they have participated to information and data. This is illustrated in the following figure:

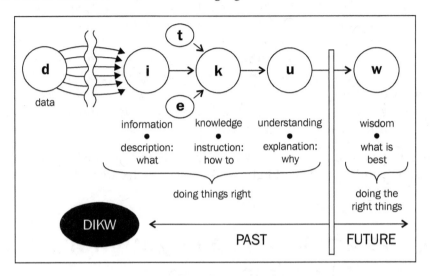

The authors' SharePoint wisdom provides insight for the reader to increase their effectiveness with SharePoint decision making process.

Example: The .NET developer

A few years ago, one of the authors was consulting at a government department in New York and working with a newly hired CIO who asked his team to assist with their first SharePoint implementation. SharePoint had just been deployed and a few small applications were complete, and they wanted technical knowledge transfer to their .NET developer so that they could take ownership of the technology and the on-going maintenance. At this point in the deployment, there was no custom development.

He was the only resource they had and concerns over single developer/ administrator fell on deaf ears. The developer, who had no administration skills with limited SharePoint knowledge became the department's technical point of contact and product evangelist.

Prior to training, we informed the developer that he needed to read a 500-page SQL server book on SQL server and a 100-page installation manual that we had written to help him (even though SharePoint had already been installed in their environment and the developer would probably not be using this skill in the near future). After the training the developer had a lot of knowledge of the backend SharePoint technology, but little practical implementation skills of the technology.

Three months after the engagement, the author was called in by the CIO and was asked to review a project that had been deployed in the SharePoint environment.

Well, you can imagine, the developer had developed a wonderful .NET solution for the SharePoint platform. However the forms, workflows, and security features that were in the application were all custom developed and could all have been deployed out of the box in SharePoint, in probably a fraction of the time and be more easily supported (if they had someone with basic end user SharePoint knowledge).

This is unfortunate for the developer, because he was a contractor and probably felt that he had to build a solution with his skill set or he would be replaced. But you have to admire his mind set, "Don't worry, I can do it."

 Remember, Google searches are no replacement for experience or a quality text book on a subject.

Shortly after this meeting, the author did hear back from the developer as he was asking about how to make the content on SharePoint externally available to users, without a VPN connection. The author was asked about his **IIS (Internet Information Services)** skills. There was a long pause on the phone and the sound of a few keyboard strokes; presumably a Google search occurred. His response was, "Don't worry, I can do it."

 In reality, this project, like other SharePoint projects, was set up to fail because of a lack of understanding of the technology, people skills, and business requests.

The CIO is no longer with this organization. This may or may not be related to this SharePoint project. You can only speculate.

This experience is personally frustrating to witness because it impacted careers and undermines the reputation that SharePoint can add real business value to an organization. So if situations like this can be avoided, it is a winner for everyone.

[Our best customer is an educated one. So read this book.]

How to use this book

Our advice is simple. Read the book from cover to cover. It should be a quick read. Please feel free to make notes of the functions and any familiar process takeaways, and use post-it notes to label important techniques to which you want to refer. In fact, mark it up with a pen and think about how to apply the answers to an upcoming SharePoint initiative, where to do some further research on a topic, or discuss with other co-workers and team members to share and exchange ideas.

This book is designed to be a primer to understanding the SharePoint technology and how to deploy and support it and not to be an endpoint to your SharePoint learning process.

What this book covers

Chapter 1, Defining a SharePoint IT Strategy, outlines the first broad process of solving business problems with the SharePoint technology and to fully understand the magnitude of the business issues.

Chapter 2, Just Enough Governance, bridges the gap between the uncontrolled environment so often seen with a SharePoint environment, and the approval and documentation-heavy processes you see in other business areas. It introduces the topic of governance in such a way that most business executives and IT leadership understand inform the readers that SharePoint can be governed just like every other platform.

Chapter 3, Deployment Roadmap, gives readers the appropriate introductory knowledge to aid them in deciding how to go about installing or upgrading SharePoint within their organizations. With a myriad of available versions and deployment options including on-premise, hosted, and cloud-based, business executives need to know what their options are, what their concerns should be, and what criteria to use to best choose the optimal venue for their SharePoint deployment.

Chapter 4, SharePoint in the Clouds, addresses important considerations for cloud-based SharePoint deployments, with a focus on Office 365 (Microsoft's premier offering) and Amazon EC2, the largest available public/private cloud. As cloud technologies mature, they are becoming more attractive to organizations for production use, and IT management needs to know the benefits and pitfalls of what the cloud can do for SharePoint.

Chapter 5, SharePoint and Important Trends, outlines IT trends that affect a SharePoint deployment in your company and educates the reader that SharePoint is not a simple application. It's an enterprise platform that is used in many different disciplines, industries, and corporate cultures. In this chapter, we explore how SharePoint is being used and leveraged within vertical markets and horizontal markets. In order to effectively determine how to invest in your SharePoint implementation, it's important to understand Microsoft's positioning, the vendor marketplace, SharePoint's competitors, and industry trends that will impact your SharePoint investments.

Chapter 6, How to get the .NET Developers on Board Quickly?, provides an approach to bring .NET developers up to speed quickly and avoid the pitfalls many other organizations have inadvertently stumbled over in the last few years. Microsoft will be the first to tell you that SharePoint is itself a .NET platform. It follows that since .NET is a mature and widely adopted technology, you'll have a rich and deep market of resources from which you can draw highly skilled SharePoint developers with minimum effort. Similarly, you may reasonably believe the same of your existing, .NET-skilled IT staff. However, you'll also quickly find that SharePoint requires your development team to acquire a fair amount of specialized knowledge.

Chapter 7, Growing SharePoint Capacity and Meeting Staffing Resource Needs, delves into what skill sets are required for SharePoint implementations, how to evaluate what your real staffing needs are, how to leverage existing resources more effectively within the organization, and how to evaluate external experts/consultants to augment your organization's capabilities. As SharePoint implementations grow and become more successful within your organization, how do you handle managing, evaluating, and acquiring the necessary talent to keep it going?

Chapter 8, Managing your First SharePoint Project, discusses criteria for selecting that "first" project, pitfalls to avoid, and best practices to follow to ensure that it's both a successful project and a template and shining example that will help your organization move forward with confidence and success with SharePoint. Many companies' first SharePoint projects fail to meet the business requirements that justified their investment in the first place, let alone provide lasting value down the road. That's a shame because it does not need to, and should not, turn out that way.

Chapter 9, Now What?, wraps up the book's objective to give the reader the ability to make positive and permanent shifts in their decision-making ability regarding SharePoint's impact and their business needs. These shifts are the direct cause for a new and unique kind of IT management perspective where the reader has the ability to further become both a SharePoint influencer and decision maker in areas that are important to them and the business.

What you need for this book

For this book to be of value, you will need an open mind to absorb and interpret the advice and experiences of the authors on the SharePoint topics that each chapter addresses. This is key, because the book's emphasis is on planning, managing, and supporting SharePoint deployments, rather than a survival step-by-step guide to a technical task.

You will also need the ability to reapply information stated in the chapter topics to SharePoint projects that you are working on or are about to be working on. This information is not always going to be 100 percent relevant to how your organization works with the SharePoint technology, so not everything should be taken literary. The authors view this information as pointers to the truth, not as the truth itself. To become an experienced manager of SharePoint deployments you must experience the truth, and not always believe it.

Who this book is for

This book is ideal to IT managers and **Line Of Business (LOB)** executives who are not hands-on with this technology. It explains the SharePoint technology in bite-size chunks, and at a technical level that is all you will need to know, yet arms you with enough knowledge to make decisions, ask further questions of your technical teams, and understand the business impact of these decisions.

This book is not designed for the developer and administrator, yet the content maybe of interest in helping provide a common vocabulary and vision between them and their lines of management.

 When discussing this book with the other writers, a strong Turkish coffee analogy was made. If techies drink strong Turkish coffee, the executives only want a distilled version of the coffee. Enough to get a feel of the flavor, make a decision, and choose whether or not to drink some more.

Conventions

In this book, you will find a number of styles of text that distinguish between different kinds of information. Here are some examples of these styles, and an explanation of their meaning.

Code words in text are shown as follows: "This framework defines the notion of a "solution" which is similar to a `.zip` file."

New terms and **important words** are shown in bold. Words that you see on the screen, in menus or dialog boxes for example, appear in the text like this: "If the demo environment is used, I highly recommend turning off features such as **Fast Search** or **Enterprise search** that are simply not used in the development experience, for the most part."

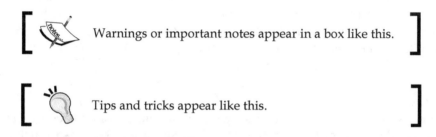

> Warnings or important notes appear in a box like this.

> Tips and tricks appear like this.

Reader feedback

Feedback from our readers is always welcome. Let us know what you think about this book—what you liked or may have disliked. Reader feedback is important for us to develop titles that you really get the most out of.

To send us general feedback, simply send an e-mail to feedback@packtpub.com, and mention the book title via the subject of your message.

If there is a book that you need and would like to see us publish, please send us a note in the **SUGGEST A TITLE** form on www.packtpub.com or e-mail suggest@packtpub.com.

If there is a topic that you have expertise in and you are interested in either writing or contributing to a book, see our author guide on www.packtpub.com/authors.

Customer support

Now that you are the proud owner of a Packt book, we have a number of things to help you to get the most from your purchase.

Errata

Although we have taken every care to ensure the accuracy of our content, mistakes do happen. If you find a mistake in one of our books—maybe a mistake in the text or the code—we would be grateful if you would report this to us. By doing so, you can save other readers from frustration and help us improve subsequent versions of this book. If you find any errata, please report them by visiting http://www.packtpub. com/support, selecting your book, clicking on the **errata submission form** link, and entering the details of your errata. Once your errata are verified, your submission will be accepted and the errata will be uploaded on our website, or added to any list of existing errata, under the Errata section of that title. Any existing errata can be viewed by selecting your title from http://www.packtpub.com/support.

Piracy

Piracy of copyright material on the Internet is an ongoing problem across all media. At Packt, we take the protection of our copyright and licenses very seriously. If you come across any illegal copies of our works, in any form, on the Internet, please provide us with the location address or website name immediately so that we can pursue a remedy.

Please contact us at copyright@packtpub.com with a link to the suspected pirated material.

We appreciate your help in protecting our authors, and our ability to bring you valuable content.

Questions

You can contact us at questions@packtpub.com if you are having a problem with any aspect of the book, and we will do our best to address it.

1
Defining a SharePoint IT Strategy

Your organization is considering whether to install SharePoint, and you are now envisioning what it can do for your company. But you also need to consider costs versus benefits, keeping in mind your company's directive of "being more strategic with IT spending". The time has come for your team to clearly define an IT strategy to guide your upcoming SharePoint deployment.

This chapter outlines a series of simple, common-sense steps to help define and implement a strategy that is aligned with the business, while simultaneously not being a huge distraction to operational work. This presents a different approach to typical "strategy sessions" which generally lead to a long-winded document, rife with complex diagrams, impressive-sounding technologies, and perhaps even some Excel clippings (with financial machinations in an attempt to give the whole thing an air of business legitimacy).

Q: Can you define what a strategy is?

A: A strategy is a plan of action designed to achieve a specific, long-term goal or result. This plan of action has explicit methods and maneuvers designed to accomplish pre-defined goals, but it can also be steered to perhaps achieve a level of differentiation against the competition, or to gain a competitive advantage. A strategy can also be implemented to guide and drive the overall aim of an organization.

The time dimension of a strategy should be subdivided into definable milestones and should include employees, shareholders, vendors, and customers. Obviously, timeframes will vary by organization and project type.

Strategies, however, are not tactical plans detailing the technical implementation of a technology your company is interested in. If your "strategy document" mentions IP addresses, networking equipment, or server farms, it's likely that your original initiative has mutated. Strategies are usually defined by senior management who do not want to be bogged down with technical details; developers and administrators generally dislike and don't participate in long strategy sessions.

A strategy could even be considered proactive observation: gathering information on the activities of specific departments, the company as a whole, the marketplace, the competition, and making decisions based on an analysis of this data.

Q: What is an IT strategy?

A: An IT strategy is a plan to achieve specific IT goals and results. In short, it is a roadmap of what, when, and why, regarding the IT ideas/initiatives that have been agreed on between the business users and IT department.

These goals should be defined by both the business and IT department. They need to balance competing objectives from multiple departments, take into consideration the breadth of the goals, prioritize them, and reclassify accordingly.

Who makes the ultimate decision on the prioritization depends on the organization's structure and internal politics. If the CTO/CIO report to the CFO, then the priorities tend to swing towards reducing costs. If the reporting structure is to the CEO, then the priorities reflect company growth. Additional priorities that may overlap into an IT strategy include marketing and brand recognition of the organization.

An IT strategy is a journey which leads to a series of milestones, perhaps defined and redefined quarterly, annually, or every five years (yes this is a long term in IT). These milestones should be shared among all senior management, employees, and contractors involved in the projects.

It is not a single meeting and a series of PowerPoint slides to impress management that are then e-mailed to a group.

> Someone senior within the organization must be accountable for the process.

For the purpose of this chapter, typical strategies could be aligned with your organizational goal, along with the assumption that most of the IT goals aid business operations.

These goals are stated in two lists as follows. The first is business-centric, whereas the second set is more IT-centric. It is how an IT strategy should be defined and implemented:

- Improve decision making
- Improve compliance for accurate records/policies for future access
- Reduce overall manpower requirements by improving efficiency
- Reduce overall risk

Other examples of goals, which could also be classified as objectives or subgoals, may include the following:

- Enable wide adoption of application
- Invest in platforms that are easier to maintain
- Reduce overall maintenance costs

Both sets of goals are equally important not just in what is actually being delivered but also in the timing of each goal.

> The most important goal is not that the SharePoint application was delivered on time, but that a user adoption level was reached at a certain point. This is a key issue with SharePoint applications.

The following figure illustrates a deployment using the strategic approach. The strategy is split into definable phases and goals with a defined end date. Notice how some of the activities (**Projects**, **Adoption**, **Organization**, **IT**, and **Infrastructure**) of the phases are split between business and IT initiatives.

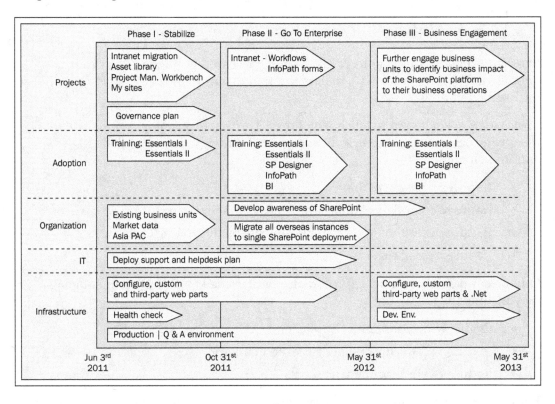

Some of the goals are continuous to the endpoint of May 2013 as illustrated. Of course, additional phases can be added to the IT strategy.

It is recommended that, at the end of each phase, a meeting should be held among IT personnel and the business to discuss the phase that has ended, identify successes, failures, and how improvements can be made for the next phase. This post mortem review process should be documented, and applied to the next steps.

Q: How do you create a SharePoint IT strategy?

A: The business and IT department need to meet and discuss objectives and capabilities. This will take more than an hour. Depending on how large the organization is, the strategy meeting would take at least a day, perhaps two and it would be beneficial to have an outside person with SharePoint expertise facilitate the discussions.

> Before embarking on an IT strategy specific to SharePoint, it would be a good idea to understand the capabilities of this technology. Before scheduling any strategy meetings, it's important to understand, at least at a high level, the value that SharePoint brings to an organization, what it takes to achieve this value in terms of time, money, and resources, and also what SharePoint will not solve or fix (such as bad business methodologies).

A typical strategy workshop should cover the following agenda:

Day 1: Diagnostics

Typical agenda for the day would be:

Intro to workshop—discussion

It will cover the following points:

- Introductions and objectives
- Workshop methodology

Company background—discussion

It will cover the following points:

- Company size and background.
- Business drivers—people, processes, and business.
- Imperatives and priorities.
- How is IT challenged? Are there legal implications and would the legal department need to be involved?

The Focus on IT environment—discussion

It will cover the following points:

- IT roles
- Projects/initiatives and applications
- Dependencies—costs, resources, services, and service levels
- IT **Strengths, Weaknesses, Opportunities,** and **Threats (SWOT)** Analysis
- Current SharePoint deployment (if this exists)

Current IT core applications—discussion

This discussion will cover the following points:

- Overview
- Availability
- Performance
- Security
- Compliance
- Mobility
- Application categories
- Ownership and control

Future IT core applications—discussion

The following points will be covered:

- Projects/initiatives and applications
- Cloud
- Third parties
- Application categories
- IT priorities
- Risks—security, compliance, performance, availability
- Overall profile

Review—discussion

At the end of the day, the workshop facilitator should write up notes for the next day. This process is similar to an ill patient visiting a doctor (Day 1) and the doctor presenting a treatment plan to the patient (Day 2).

Day 1 complete at 5:00 p.m.

Day 2: The treatment plan

Typical agenda for the day would be:

Initial findings and review—discussion

It will cover the following points:

- Application categories
- Overall profile
- Priorities risk register (SMART)
- SharePoint match
- Impact assessment
- Ownership and control
- External considerations

The Gap analysis

Gap analysis will cover:

- Technology
- People
- Processes

Priorities, actions, and agreement

It will cover:

- Risks
- Budget
- Adoption—IT, users, and business units

- Political wins
- Mapping SharePoint to business needs
- Third-party tools and customization

Review—discussion

The review covers:

- Maximizing impact (cost versus value versus number of people impacted)

Day 2 complete at 5:00 p.m.

During day 2, the group will identify in-scope applications that could be moved to the SharePoint platform, or determine whether to build them or not. This is logged on the priorities register.

 During these two days, discussions and actions occur. If decisions cannot be made during these days, they need to be made shortly after this strategy session. If this is a large company, maybe extra days are required.

The result of this could be:

Application categories - HR		
Functionality	SharePoint functionality	Biz Impact
Expense System		2
Knowledge base		2
Timesheet		2
On boarding	InfoPath forms, workflow	2
Policy Document Review	Third-party web part	2
Performance Management	InfoPath forms, workflow	2
Skill set finder	My sites	2
PDF forms on intranet	InfoPath forms, workflow	2

Bold - functionality that will not be replicated in SharePoint

The results of the ranking of the priority register is illustrated in the previous figure and the methodology of the business impact ranking process is illustrated as follows:

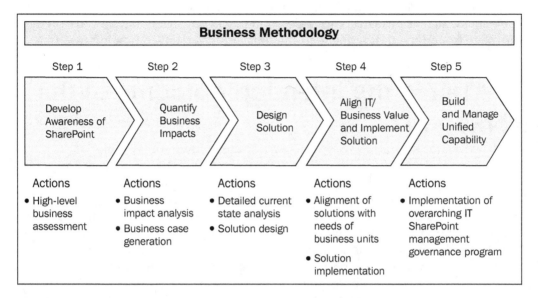

Day 3: A successful SharePoint implementation plan

Typical agenda for the day would be:

Next steps—discussion

It will cover:

- Strategy plan (strategy deployment approach figure)
- Table of actions

Summary and close out

The following points will be covered:

- Overall findings
- Outputs
- Action plan for 90-day actions

Day 3 complete at 4:00 p.m.

Your SharePoint IT strategy will also need to work in tandem with other existing IT strategies and resources, so it is important that they are synchronized with this strategy session. In addition, the strategy should be shared with other groups within the business such as infrastructure, sales, and marketing, such that they are on the same page in understanding the requirements and potential competing resources.

Q: What is the intended outcome of the workshop?

A: This workshop's findings will need to be discussed with other senior management to determine who will be the ultimate budget and resource approvers. For post-workshop conversations, the deployment roadmap approach figure at the beginning of the chapter provides a visual description of the roadmap for management's understanding, as well as a Gap Analysis. This tool identifies where your organization currently is with its SharePoint deployment, and defined future steps. The following figure is a typical Gap Analysis that shows the current and future states that relate to the organization's technology, people, and processes. It asks two core questions: "Where are we?" and "Where do we want to be?" By asking these questions, management has the opportunity to allocate resources to projects and initiatives, and to identify the gaps between goals and resource allocations.

This tool does involve determining, documenting, and approving the variance between business requirements and current capabilities.

If you wish, the Gap Analysis tool can be used to benchmark your goals with other companies and other assessments. Once the general expectation of performance in the industry is understood, it is possible to compare that expectation with the company's current level of performance.

Gap Analysis		
	Current	**Future**
Technology	An environment that works...Kind of!!	Correctly architected and scaled to business requirements
People	Administrator Solutions architect	Administrator Solutions architect Business engagement manager SharePoint evangelist
Processes	Self service model	Talk and chalk sessions Someone who can see IT as a strategic asset

Another post-workshop tool is a SWOT analysis (Strengths, Weaknesses, Opportunities, and Threats). The following figure is a SWOT analysis diagram that identifies the four components of the analysis:

SWOT Analysis	
Strengths Some technology expertise Microsoft complementary products MS enterprise licenses Reduction of third-party applications	**Opportunities** Richer user experience of workday Clean slate to start
Weaknesses Office versions not 2010 Supporting live environment	**Threats** Scalability and planning Fully defined governance plan

Management often loves these figures because they are good talking points for members of the workshop and are definable and actionable for the teams.

Q: Who needs to be involved with the process?

A: A variety of organizational personnel will be involved in the development, execution, and analysis of any IT strategy at different times.

The key to success is the input from IT and business management who have the ability and authority to assign resources to the project, and to authorize business initiatives as they relate to SharePoint.

Because a strategy is not a single project, there generally is not a single business sponsor, but rather senior members from both the IT and business sides of the organization. To increase the chances of success, these individuals should be involved from the beginning of the strategy defining process. The business sponsor is responsible for communicating the overall objectives they seek to accomplish with the assistance of IT. During this dialogue, the IT sponsor is responsible for understanding the high-level feasibility and risk as well as the desired functionality; this is the Risk Registry. Once these items are understood, the IT sponsor will need to come back with the proposed IT strategy to meet these goals. It is the IT sponsor's responsibility to understand the resources required to ensure successful execution of the IT strategy. Initial resources to consider may include IT personnel, operational personnel, and helpdesk personnel.

Your advocates may come from various disciplines. A good place to start would be the management teams of those individuals most likely to benefit from the prioritized list. However, do not forget resources that help to drive the adoption and solicit feedback once your solution is live.

If you work in the IT department, you may witness continuous requests for IT resources or initiatives with the SharePoint platform for business users. This is good, because they see you or your department as a strategic asset that can help them solve problems. If this is the case, then some of these requestors should attend the SharePoint workshop or at least see the post-workshop findings.

If you work in the IT department and the business community in your organization does not make requests, then there is a chance your department is not viewed as a strategic asset and you may be even viewed as an operational cost. If this is the case, the workshop is an opportunity to bring perceived value to the business.

Funny you should say that...

Up to this part of the chapter the reader has been introduced to a process of how to define an IT strategy for SharePoint for their business. This section of the chapter answers questions that the reader may now have about how to apply knowledge from this chapter to their organization.

Q: Do I need to get the CEO involved?

A: A typical IT strategy does not require the CEO's hands-on involvement. However, an IT strategy, at the end of the day, truly serves only the corporate strategy.

Ultimately, there is really only one true strategic player in the organization: the CEO and his or her counterparts on the board. All the other officers of the corporation must use their respective departments to help the CEO execute the company's strategy. Most business units align their activities to the corporate strategy and similarly, IT must wrap its strategy around the business's.

Therefore, by all means, share your finding with the CEO to demonstrate that your department is supporting the corporate strategy. Most CEOs care about dominating a market or increasing sales and not necessarily whether or not you have a deployment plan for any product. So the last thing you really want is a non-technical person being very influential with an IT strategy that they don't understand.

Q: Why is a SharePoint strategy different than other IT products?

A: It is because SharePoint is a platform. It can be difficult to define the functionality that has or could have been deployed to the business, so the milestones/endpoints are different than those for a typical application such as a CRM system.

Also for a SharePoint strategy to become a deployment reality, there are several dependent technologies that SharePoint relies on, which need to be in place and set up correctly for the initiatives to work. For example, user profile synchronization needs to be configured appropriately with **Active Directory** in order for the organization chart in **My Sites** to work.

 You will read "SharePoint is a platform" endlessly throughout this book. So what does this mean? A platform has multiple functionality that can be applied to different applications such as search, workflow, document management and content management, and .NET development, which takes time to configure and deploy within an organization.

An application is like Microsoft Word, a program that is very clearly defined for the single purpose of writing documentation. As stated many times in this book, SharePoint is a platform for web applications to be developed on.

This is why SharePoint can be difficult to define and describe to people. Another term you will hear is that it is the Swiss Army knife of Microsoft's web offerings, because the tool has many blades.

Microsoft will often explain SharePoint with the pin wheel, which is illustrated as follows:

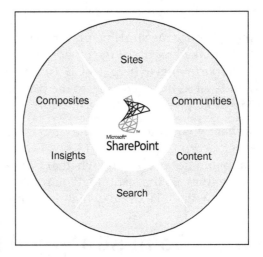

Given SharePoint's broad functionality and its potential to be used by any employee in an organization, defining a strategy can be a challenge. This is unlike a Customer Relationship application where generally only the sales and marketing departments are involved and processes are already defined.

Another reason why defining a SharePoint strategy is unique is because employees may have had an experience with SharePoint at a previous job, and want to repeat this experience again. What they often do not realize is that their previous experience may have consisted of a customized SharePoint environment, or one augmented with third-party components. These employees end up surprised and disappointed when their expectations don't comply with the current deployment.

It is essential to educate the user community about SharePoint if you really want to leverage it's functionality. It is important to gauge the level of interest and time that business users have and are willing to spend on SharePoint awareness.

Q: What are the pitfalls of a SharePoint strategy?

A: The biggest pitfall would be to neglect involvement of the business in forming an IT business strategy.

If IT attempts to create its own "strategy" centered on technology, there will be a problem. A division between IT and the rest of the organization will increase as most other business units have aligned their activities to the corporate strategy.

 The name of the game is for an IT strategy to support the corporate strategy.

It's a bit like the used car salesman trying to peddle the high-margin two-seater sports car on the lot, despite the fact that the customer explicitly mentions a wife, three kids, and the 80-pound family dog. The salesperson may have a deep mastery of the technical and aesthetic attributes of the sports car, but his "strategy" is at odds with the customer, no matter how knowledgeable he is about the product or how it could be applied to the customer's problem.

As a technologist and business person, you can avoid these pitfalls by marrying technologies with the corporate strategy and keeping in mind that a successfully executed strategic objective is more important than the tools used to get there. Yes, this may mean that .NET development may have to wait. This mindset adds a healthy dose of pragmatism to IT and aligns IT with the rest of the organization and brings a results-oriented focus to IT.

Rather than cooking up ROI numbers, or attempting to assign a "business benefit" to the cost of sending a single e-mail, this mindset puts IT in the business strategy and produces or enables business results and can be seen as a true business partner.

Thus you can begin to see that business involvement is crucial for validation of goal, approach, and partnership during the development and go-live phases. Once the business is involved, you can set a path for success and most of the remaining pitfalls can be avoided with effective project management.

Planning pitfalls may include aspects such as failing to schedule well-defined project milestones. Specific to IT planning, having the right skill sets in place is critical. This is where experience and up-to-date training will pay dividends. Take time to identify gaps in knowledge or experience. As long as the void in skills is identified, you can plan around it with a combination of training and outsourcing. Otherwise, you risk embarking on a very expensive training exercise and possible project failure.

"Scope creep" is another common pitfall when dealing with IT projects. It's common to come up with additional ideas on how IT technology can be applied. The challenge will be to decide how to track and accommodate requests for changes in scope. As project budgets and timelines are established at the beginning of the project, it is important to incorporate a methodology on how to respond to scope changes up front as well.

Knowing how to say no or when to push back is a great trait to avoid this pitfall. Having too rich a functional goal mixed with a delivery timeline that is too ambitious will set you up for falling far short of expectations. By keeping business values top of your mind, you will be able to make the right trade-off in this area.

Another common pitfall with an IT strategy is failing to properly accommodate for dependencies. These dependencies vary from needed resources (hardware, personnel) to availability of system interaction (parallel IT projects, test data, migration windows of opportunity, and so on). As is the case with skill sets, take time at the commencement of the project and strategic milestones to check your dependencies and have a contingency plan where needed. Of course this does not help when a five-year strategy is at the mercy of the yearly budget review.

Adoption is also often overlooked while considering IT business strategy because it is easy for IT personnel to neglect adoption. This is because they will undoubtedly know more on how to use the system or application because they built it and they may fall in love with their own project while forgetting to put themselves in the shoes of the end user and business management. IT adoption can be aided with a mix of proper training, evangelizing, and desire to understand the business.

Lastly, it is important to remember that an IT business strategy is more of a journey than a destination. Just as business needs evolve, the technology that we can apply to aiding the business seems to evolve even quicker. With this in mind, your knowledge of the IT world should always be growing and your methodologies should constantly be refreshed.

Q: Why do we really need an IT strategy?

A: In short, the strategy will help prioritize IT efforts to support the business requests. The key aspect of an IT strategy is to manage expectations of both the business and IT department so that both parties know what to expect and when.

In the first figure of the chapter, there is a clear roadmap of SharePoint deliverables for the business so budgets can be defined and resources allocated. The details of how this is done do not necessarily need to be agreed upon in the strategy meeting. In fact, given that the budget is not defined at the workshop, some initiatives may not be feasible.

By having an IT strategy for SharePoint, return on investment can be identified with some effort and initiatives being approved and prioritized.

Without a strategy, there is normally a passive approach to a SharePoint deployment, where initiatives are not coordinated among departments and low value processes are used with SharePoint, such as fancier and more expensive set of shared drives rather than a usable ECM system with findable information assets.

Research by AIIM stated that half of SharePoint implementations proceed without a clear business case (which shows lack of direction from the start); only 22 percent of the organizations provide users with any guidance on corporate classification and use of content types and columns; one third of the organizations have no plans as to how to use SharePoint, while one fourth of the organizations say IT is driving it with no input from information management professionals.

Digging deeper

This section of the chapter outlines areas of an IT strategy that the reader may wish to know more about.

Q: Any final words of advice on this?

A: Rushing off to "the next big thing" after completing a phase or a project of the first phase of the strategy road map is a bad idea. But even in the most successful projects, there are usually items still remaining. Additionally, after a few weeks or months "in the wild," the people using the fruits of your labor may have some great and often simple-to-implement ideas for improvement. However, the project is complete, deployed to the specified scope, and your resources are working on another project.

This problem often happens with SharePoint projects, when phase II functionality is urgently required to meet business expectations and perhaps prevent an initiative stalling, yet the additional resources and perhaps an already large investment of time and money is allocated to other projects.

This is typical of SharePoint projects partly because the end user actually knows what they really want, once they realize that they have to use SharePoint and experience what they requested.

In short, a small additional effort can have dramatic effects, accelerating and amplifying results. Therefore, you may want to factor in a six-month revisit on projects and should not be afraid to move projects out of phases, or even eliminate them if the business value will be trumped by a phase II project.

Often IT will say to the business this is the initial foundation for future growth, but if you allow the project team, momentum, and leadership to scatter, never to return again, the effort and time of building that complex foundation is reduced to nothing. SharePoint deployments like other deployments require a support team.

Summary

In this chapter you have been guided on how to create a SharePoint strategy for your organization, and been shown the information and actions that are produced after the strategy workshop.

The strategy challenges and pitfalls were also explained.

This is the first chapter of the book and has given the reader the knowledge to begin to explore SharePoint deployments within an organization. We recommend that you review this chapter again once you have read all the other chapters of the book so you are fully aware of the deployment strategies, and what is needed to staff your resources and build capacity, and ultimately have a successful SharePoint deployment that delivers business results.

2
Just Enough Governance

In a time when executives are requesting iPads and iPhones as part of standard issued IT equipment, "SharePoint Governance" can be seen as a boring phrase, but nevertheless it is an important one. This is especially true when businesses are increasingly betting their livelihood and reputation on the latest technology.

In almost every failed SharePoint deployment we have witnessed, the main reasons are lack of governance or poor governance, weak leadership, or uninformed managers. This chapter bridges the gap between the uncontrolled environments so often seen with a SharePoint engagement, and the endless approval sign-off process requirement you see in other business areas.

By the end of this chapter, through the format of various questions and answers, you will have been introduced to how to apply governance to your SharePoint deployment with a balanced approach, which we are calling "Just enough governance". This approach is eye opening for many senior IT executives who are normally confronted by the amount of required governance for IT deployments. This is because with traditional IT deployments, the focus is on governance such as **data storage, farms,** and **development,** rather than end-user activity and content.

Although end users cannot normally crash a SharePoint application with their activity, if they view SharePoint as difficult to use and having limited functionality, partly because user activity and content management have not been defined within governance and they are vocal, then further SharePoint initiatives from business units could be a challenge.

This is why a governance approach is required to cover the entire SharePoint community within the organization to ensure effective and efficient use of SharePoint, thus enabling an organization to achieve its business strategy goals.

Q. What is governance?

A: Governance is defined as "the processes that need to be followed in order to achieve a successful department, team, or project". In the case of IT, governance is the administering of IT resources by the processes of planning, prioritization, decision-making, and performance measurement.

Often governance is already occurring in your department, but it is not formally written down. True IT governance is this process written down, followed through and reviewed by a governance committee, in other words, a formalization of the current process.

In essence you are creating a state of control, which prevents people from following bad paths, and are forcing them through the process that you define, such as training, and proper documentation to follow the right path.

Q. Why do we need it?

A: The number one answer is "buy-in". If IT and business want to become true partners, or even if you don't and just want people to go along quietly with your advice, you need to make them part of the process. Much of our success with IT is dependent on users, management, and stakeholders buying into the solutions such as SharePoint and then IT guides them. No buy-in often leads to failure.

Q: So where do I start with governance?

A: Good question. First, remember that governance is a continuing process and not a "one-shot deal", where a great deal of documentation is produced, reviewed, and updated. Where to start does depend on your current SharePoint strategy, as discussed in the previous chapter. If your organization is new to SharePoint, we suggest that you identify the most basic areas that are required to be governed, such as:

- IT—service level agreements, enterprise applications, application owners, budgets, and database management
- Internal/external end users in terms of security and training
- Development—release policies, technical documentation, and support
- Infrastructure—backup and restore procedures, server names, and authentication
- Training
- Security—who can edit content and make changes to infrastructure

These documents could even start off as guidelines that only have the sections defined and state why they are blank.

These areas are stated as follows:

- IT
- End user
- Development—.Net development
- Infrastructure

In the previous bullet points, it is assumed that .Net development work is being performed with the SharePoint implementation. If this is not the case, then the governance policy does not need to include development.

 Only write policies that relate to activities within your existing SharePoint environment. This will save effort in writing and maintaining policies and give the reader an opportunity to provide feedback to the author, because they are using it for guidance for their work.

People always ask about development governance when they look at other governance documentation, so you could even write a development document and state in the first paragraph:

Because development is not envisioned for another 12 months, this document is incomplete.

Over time, as the SharePoint technology becomes widely adopted within the organization, governance documentation will grow to cover other activities such as:

- Infrastructure—server builds, naming conventions, disaster recovery, and release policies
- Project management—type of projects and user base for project management
- Content management—versions, metadata and document types such as corporate policies
- Social Networking 2.0—blogging, MySites, and wikis
- Security—SharePoint permissions and access inheritance

Unless you are required to use a corporate policy document template, we recommend that you have a separate document for each policy, rather than a huge 500 page document that might be perceived as overwhelming to the average user. This will make the policies much easier to develop and manage, as well as for the end user to read and absorb.

We live in a corporate world where people rarely read documentation anymore. By making information more bite size and relevant, it increases the chance of the document making it from the printer to the reader.

It does not mean that vital details of a policy should be omitted just because of short attention spans.

Each document should state the following, and have a similar structure:

- Related document(s)
- Target reader
- What's in it for the reader
- Owner of the policy
- Policies and procedures of subject
- Expiration of the policy

The expiration of the policy is particularly important, because nothing undermines the policy more than outdated information. A good way to write policy documents is to review the governance documents that have already been written for the organization and verify existing governance documents' structure and content.

The following link shows a sample template of the SharePoint Products and Technologies governance plan:

```
http://waterbillhubbell.web.officelive.com/Documents/EXAMPLE,%20
SharePoint%202010%20Governance%20Plan,%20Bill%20Hubbell,%20Oct%20
2010.pdf.
```

Q: Who should be involved with SharePoint governance?

A: It is important for a governance committee to be involved and engaged. The committee should meet on a regular basis to discuss the topic of SharePoint governance with the management team; everything from IT infrastructure, line businesses, and application development (part of the SharePoint steering committee).

An IT steering committee is a governance body that reviews, monitors, and prioritizes major IT projects from a cross-functional perspective. The two key concerns of a technology steering committee are as follows:

- Alignment: The committee helps ensure that IT strategy is aligned with the strategic goals of the organization

- Ownership: The business units represented on the steering committee have ultimate ownership over the larger IT strategic decisions, since those decisions will impact their processes

The top three activities of IT steering committees are IT project prioritization, approval of IT projects, and IT strategic planning.

A steering committee has a broader objective than a governance committee.

This is illustrated in the following figure:

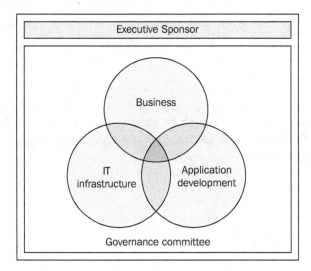

The previous figure illustrates how a governance committee can serve as a mechanism that balances power and influence between the various constituents. Each overlaps the other equally.

This committee should be overseen by a senior officer of the company who has the authority to bring parties together.

 It is a *big* mistake to limit governance conversations to only IT personnel, because a governance policy has to be adhered to and understood by all stakeholders of an application.

Case study: Include everyone

This example discusses a SharePoint intranet site for a Catholic hospital and how it is important to include all parties of the organization when setting up governance.

The hospital had set up a governance committee to oversee the governance of content, user activity, and IT. After months of requirement gathering and development, the committee had talented project managers and infrastructure personnel on the team who were all very excited about this new technology, which could make content more up-to-date and targeted to users.

Within two days, the site was shut down.

The intranet site included information on stem cell research and birth control.

The governance committee failed to have any clergy representation on the committee and overlooked governance of content, an important consideration given the nature of the organization and its clients.

This is just one example where external considerations were not thought about during the content management process. Think about other laws and regulatory and compliance bodies such as **Health Insurance Portability and Accountability Act (HIPPA)** and **Securities and Exchange Commission (SEC)**, which audit organizations' IT operations.

Q: Is it worth hiring a consulting firm to create your company's governance documentation?

A: The authors of this book are all consultants within the SharePoint industry, and all agree the answer to the question in most cases is "No…Not to do all the work". The only result is that you simply end up outsourcing the problem to a third party.

One of the problems with hiring a consulting firm is that you are paying for them to produce the documentation, rather than taking the time and effort to understand your own business. Understanding the business would be part of the consulting engagement; but ultimately for governance to work, someone within the organization needs to take ownership of the policies and make sure they are workable, and that IT, the businesses, and users adhere to them. This is an ongoing process and should be a continuing process long after the consultants have gone.

Work with a consulting firm that has experience of SharePoint governance, with the understanding that you should not outsource the effort completely. In many ways, by hiring a consulting firm you are paying for someone to sit down, understand processes that you already know, and put these into words that will look pretty in PowerPoint, rather than actually working with a group to apply a best-practices approach to your organization, which can be regularly reviewed and be an ongoing activity.

A good consulting company will help you get started. Try telling someone to "create governance" and assess the progress. This consulting firm is guiding the governance process, identifying gaps in the documentation, and confirming policies are acceptable in the organization.

"Just enough governance" is not a job title or a qualification. It is an approach that is initiated by a leader and one that your teams adhere to. It is similar to leadership — difficult to define, but you know it when you see it.

Q: Why does it seem that SharePoint requires more governance than other technologies?

A: This is partly because SharePoint is not a strictly defined product with a clearly defined beginning and endpoint in terms of user behavior, content, and IT deployment.

SharePoint is like a "Swiss Army knife" of application platforms that has extreme versatility, so it does not fit neatly into one single software category in terms of its definition, functionality, or user approach. It also means that a company's investment in SharePoint can deliver more than just a "document management system" to the organization, and can also replace website technology, intranets, bespoke applications, and network drives. So SharePoint governance must be relevant to the user base and functionality, which will be different in different organizations because there could be a different deployment approach, other complementary technologies, and end users.

For example, a CRM system is pretty clearly defined. The user base is typically a sales force, the content is sales data, and the reports are dashboards.

Conversely, with a SharePoint implementation, the purposes could be any of the following:

- Business intelligence, for example, KPIs
- Social computing — wikis, blogs, and so on
- Communities — rating, comments, tagging, and so on
- Composites with business integration with Access, Visio, and Excel
- Advanced document management — "One version of the truth", with version control and alert notifications
- Easy-to-understand collaboration for non-technical people
- Workflows
- Information discovery and so on

One simple analogy is that SharePoint is like a huge box of Lego from the local toy store. When you get those huge sets, there's no picture of what it's going to build, as that's totally up to you. If you're careful, creative, and plan well, you can build a castle, an airplane, or even a rocket ship. Or, if you're not as good, you (sadly) get a pretty big sized brick of little pieces that does nothing and represents even less.

A governance plan is required to build the rocket ship.

The user base could be internal/external users or even non-corporate employees, and this could change over time. The content can range from text and Office documents, to media videos.

We have not addressed release procedures or branding, which can also be a huge focus point for governance, because these areas are huge and would probably require their own governance book to do justice to them. For further information, visit the following link:

```
http://www.sharepointpromag.com/article/
sharepoint/sharepoint-branding-101-how-to-
implement-a-custom-branded-site-129843.
```

Any SharePoint governance documents that expect to have any chance of being read and adhered to, at the very least, must cover the user base of the activity that is being addressed in the document, and the technically involved business groups, such as infrastructure and development.

What is key to a successful SharePoint deployment is user adoption. However, because a SharePoint application is sometimes not clearly defined in terms of what it can and cannot do, the user and businesses require clearly defined parameters in content, training, and service level agreements. The governance we are recommending strikes a balance in what businesses and the user community require and expect, as well as what IT can support. So it is vital that all parties that are reading and writing governance documents have some conversations prior to the governance policies being finalized.

Since SharePoint normally replaces or complements an existing process such as e-mail or another system, end-user awareness of dos and don'ts, as well as clarity of the SharePoint process, content, and procedures are all key for governance to succeed.

Funny you should say that...

This section explains some typical follow up questions you may have once you start to think about governance and how to begin with writing policies and procedures.

Q: How do you define "just enough governance"?

A: This will vary depending on the organization and industry. For readers who are within the IT industry, your job is business-driven by the following four goals:

- Making sure IT is aligned to the organization's business needs. Or even better, making sure IT is acting as part of the business and is not seen as an outsider.

- Delivering IT to the business.

- Managing IT risks at acceptable levels.

- Complying with IT external regulations.

To apply these goals with this balance of "just enough governance", your mantra should be:

- **Go slow to go fast**: You will succeed more quickly in the end if you don't try to govern everything all at once.

- **Prioritize**: Get the SharePoint enterprise mission-critical application into a governance framework, and leave the department contact directory for another day. For further information, review the previous chapter.

Q: How do I strike this so-called "balance"?

A: This is an easy mantra for consultants to preach, and more challenging for you to implement.

We recommend that you start off with a set of governance documents that are simple to read and understand.

Chapter 2

 Remember that policies must provide value (direction). If they don't, remove them from any documentation.

People often throw in too much governance and there are simply too many forms to fill out and meetings to attend. Because of this, there is no workability among the stakeholders and policies are not followed, or individuals are very vocal about the red tape, and that it takes too long to implement anything. Don't be afraid of removing policies that don't work or that won't add value to the business. If there is no .Net development occurring, why have a .Net governance policy document?

Q: Well, we have got this far without governance with SharePoint, so why bother?

A: My response to you would be, "Is SharePoint being used for mission-critical enterprise-wide applications?" If the answer is yes, then you are living on borrowed time.

Organizations that have mission-critical IT applications running their business, are betting on this technology to grow their business, outperform the competition, or assist a sales team in closing deals. If these systems do not work, there are serious questions to be asked by all parties involved. These questions are normally, "Why did this happen?", "How do we fix it?", "Could this have been this be avoided?" and so on.

These questions are usually not faced when you have a clearly relevant and strongly adhered to governance policy. However, good governance policies will not always prevent issues, because you are dealing with the unpredictability factor of people not just reading documents, but also misreading information.

Although you may say that you have no governance, in reality you probably do. The knowledge and "guidelines" are just not written down on paper, and are roaming around the corridors of the building, or verbally communicated. This informal, but often quite common practice won't save you when that employee leaves the organization and takes this knowledge with them. or when you've been notified that you will be having the pleasure of being audited by internal and/or external auditors.

If the answer is no, then your organization is probably only using minimal SharePoint functionality to aim its business processes, and the technology is not being viewed as a strategic asset for their operations.

The definition of a mission-critical application would be a system in which it is absolutely necessary to meet a major organization objective, for example, NASA, where mission-critical elements were those items that had to work, otherwise the billion-dollar space mission would blow up. Key point: A big problem with corporations is that they do not spend enough time hardening mission-critical applications, or spend too much effort on non-mission-critical elements.

Q: Our existing governance plan hasn't improved deployments or reduced frustrations; any suggestions?

A: In this case, the governance you have in place is not working. You should step in and do something about it, particularly if SharePoint is an enterprise-wide application. If this is not done, often what occurs is that a non-technical Director steps in and applies a heavy-handed governance approach that normally ends up being a box-ticking exercise, having people perform irrelevant steps that don't produce results.

This rule-based approach may produce policies where forms are beautifully filled in, but in reality provides minimal value.

Try to identify the following about your governance:

- What is working?
- What is not working?
- What is not working as well as it should?

To get these questions answered is a challenge, because governance is seen as a low priority and from the author's experience, if you go looking for volunteers for this, either everyone gets a sudden call to another meeting, or you find a real ball buster with a hidden agenda who is looking to make a stink and piss everybody off. Be extremely careful when you ask for this — you might be letting a fox loose in the henhouse.

Assign someone accountable to the governance polices and processes, and be sure to review the previous points quarterly with the executive sponsor, relevant business users, and technical users of the specific policy. Areas that are normally discussed are:

- New areas where SharePoint is now being considered to be used with support procedures
- Content that may require governance to be applied
- User security
- New governance practices that new team members have experienced in previous organizations

Over time, identify areas where improvement is required and set goals to achieve those improvements.

 This quarterly meeting should have lively discussion, and perhaps even disagreement. If the meeting is a "weather report", then this could be a sign that there is something wrong with the existing governance policies.

Q: Won't governance slow down the speed of innovation?

A: No. Governance is not the enemy of innovation; rather the bridge across that allows you to access it. If you can establish reliable applications in SharePoint that are supported and appear to be proactively managed, business managers will understand the additional steps to a successful SharePoint deployment and will expect this with their initiatives, because the chance of success is far greater.

With this new confidence, business managers will start pushing the boundaries of the technology and perhaps think outside the box, with the belief that the governance policies will catch potential system failures.

Digging deeper

Now you are probably thinking where governance can be applied to your existing or upcoming SharePoint implementation and require some resources to begin the process. This section states some reputable recommended sites.

Q: Where can I find further information on a governance approach with SharePoint?

A: In a perfect world, there is a 40 page governance document that is ideal for your organization and can be downloaded for free. In the real world, this is impossible because so much depends on your SharePoint environment, user base, and business initiatives and where you are establishing a governance policy.

There is a lot of information available online about SharePoint governance. The following are some suggested useful links, which will help to get you started:

- `http://technet.microsoft.com/en-us/library/cc263356.aspx`
- `http://technet.microsoft.com/en-us/library/cc262943%28office.12%29.aspx`
- `http://www.office.microsoft.com/download/afile.aspx?AssetID=AM102306291033`
- `http://www.microsoft.com/download/en/details.aspx?displayLang=en&id=401`
- `http://technet.microsoft.com/en-us/library/ff848257.aspx`
- `http://www.itgi.org/`

These links are good starting points to governance and expand on the questions and answers presented in this chapter, but there is no replacement for sitting down, writing, and discussing documents with colleagues, and engaging in the business with *just enough governance*.

Summary

In this chapter, questions and answers about SharePoint governance have provided insight into what and how governance can be applied to the SharePoint technology, with the *just enough governance* approach.

The trick is to tame SharePoint deployments and not break the spirit, so a balance is required between the user, IT, and the business.

The next chapter explains where to install the SharePoint technology. The governance considerations for this IT decision should extend not only to SharePoint governance, but also the IT security policy or hosted technology, and as well as content that is stored in the cloud.

3
Deployment Roadmap

After deciding on a business strategy and getting a rudimentary handle on governance, it's time to dive deeper into the SharePoint space. You've attended conferences, online Q&A sessions, and watched free promotional demos. You've probably even had consulting firms present their solutions, tailored to the needs of your firm. With this much research, you think you have pretty much figured out SharePoint. It's no longer just a hot buzzword or some abstract platform. It's tangible and you're ready to start deploying.

But do you really know enough about the technical side of the SharePoint landscape? Have you mapped the real hardware and software requirements for your organization, and their associated costs?

The functionality and usability requirements that you identify will ultimately drive the architectural decisions that you make. At the very least, you need to know enough to be able to effectively brainstorm a versatile architecture with your technical staff. You will need to oversee and align their technical efforts to ensure they are able to deliver the system that you have envisioned and promised to your company and its employees.

This chapter dissects the general concepts that you need to know, by focusing on ten critical questions that you should be asking to help get your deployment plan off the ground. Understanding these concepts will prepare you to make the right decisions including:

- Which SharePoint edition to choose?
- How to handle licensing?
- How to handle authentication for end users?

By the time you've finished reading this chapter, you will know what to look for, what decisions you'll need to make, and common pitfalls that you would do well to avoid. With the answers to the right questions, you'll be able to spearhead this deployment and make the optimal choices for your organization.

Q: Which edition of SharePoint is right for me?

A: SharePoint is currently a fourth-generation product and, as such, has gone through quite a few name and edition changes over the years. In its last incarnation, the two general variants of the platform were referred to as **Microsoft Office SharePoint Server 2007 (MOSS 2007)** and **Windows SharePoint Services v3 (WSSv3)**. The newest release, SharePoint 2010 comes in a variety of new flavors, and it is essential that you understand the differences between the editions and what each edition offers. The SharePoint editions expose different feature sets, so you need to know what features you are interested in offering to your user base.

SharePoint comes in three main editions, and the feature sets are cumulative:

- SharePoint Foundation
- SharePoint Server 2010 Standard
- SharePoint Server 2010 Enterprise

The different SharePoint 2010 editions also require different licenses, so determining your optimal configuration early will save you time and headache when it comes to your expectations concerning licensing costs. SharePoint 2010 licensing is addressed later on in this chapter.

SharePoint Foundation

The direct successor to WSSv3, SharePoint Foundation continues to be offered as a free product. SharePoint Foundation introduces your organization to team sites, collaborative content in lists and libraries, web parts, wikis, blogs, RSS feeds, alerts, Microsoft Office integration, and browser-based customization. SharePoint Foundation also allows you to work with external data through **Business Connectivity Services**, and exposes **Claims-Based Authentication** as an additional method of connecting to corporate identity systems. This is an entry-level offering, best suited to individual departments or organizations eager to step into the SharePoint space without making significant financial commitments.

SharePoint Server 2010 Standard

The Standard Edition picks up where SharePoint Foundation left off, by extending the core feature set to include social networking, compliance and governance capabilities, enterprise-scale search, and advanced web and enterprise content management. Standard introduces many additional modules including **Word Automation Services** for document rendering and manipulation, and the **Managed Metadata Service**, to centrally define and manage corporate metadata. It is ideal for organizations that are ready to start standardizing and consolidating business processes, with SharePoint as their nexus of integration and presentation.

Please note that while upgrades from SharePoint Foundation 2010 to SharePoint Server 2010 are supported, they can be cumbersome and complex. It is much easier to gather the correct requirements initially, and start with the right edition, rather than having to re-architect and migrate at a later date. More information on SharePoint Server 2010 upgrades and upgrade paths can be found on the Microsoft website (`http://technet.microsoft.com/en-us/library/cc303429.aspx`).

SharePoint Server 2010 Enterprise

The Enterprise Edition is considered the premium product, and focuses on adding business intelligence, integration and reporting, along with advanced search capability. Enterprise also includes additional Microsoft Office client services, namely, Access, Excel, InfoPath, PerformancePoint, and Visio services, and paves the way for advanced search scalability and extensibility. Enterprise edition is geared for organizations that have moved beyond using SharePoint for operations; it has become a strategic platform.

FAST Search Server 2010 for SharePoint 2010

Although not one of the true "core" SharePoint editions, FAST Search Server is worth mentioning as a valuable addition to both SharePoint Server 2010 Standard and Enterprise Edition platforms. FAST is a high-end set of search tools designed to enhance the search experience and also a platform for building search-driven applications. FAST Search Server brings lots of new functionality including phonetic search, thumbnails and previews, visual search, and best bets. A well publicized deployment was done at General Mills, one of the world's leading food companies, which deployed FAST to create a comprehensive, tunable search-driven application focused on the needs of the firm's researchers. The case study can be found at `http://www.microsoft.com/casestudies/Microsoft-FAST-Search-Server-2010-For-Sharepoint/General-Mills/General-Mills-Frees-More-Time-for-Innovation-with-Research-Focused-Search-Application/4000007255`.

The following figure highlights key features of the different SharePoint editions. Note that the features are cumulative, so the Enterprise Edition includes all Foundation and Standard features.

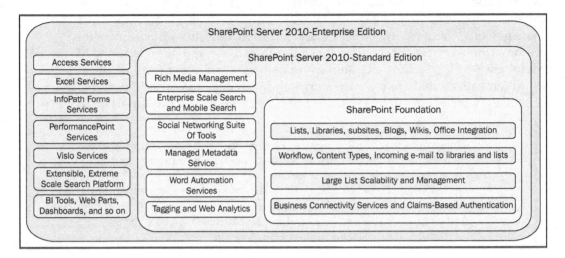

There are a few other editions that are often mentioned, but their difference primarily revolves around licensing, not functionality. These include the following:

- SharePoint Server 2010 for Internet Sites, Standard
- SharePoint Server 2010 for Internet Sites, Enterprise
- Office 365
- FAST Search Server 2010 for Internet Sites

SharePoint Server 2010 for Internet Sites, Standard

With the success of SharePoint as an intranet, many firms also opt to use SharePoint for their public Internet presence. The **For Internet Sites (FIS)** edition of the product provides the same features corresponding to SharePoint Server 2010 Standard Edition, but with the intention of being used directly on the Internet. The objective of the Standard Edition is to enable firms to get a SharePoint web presence off the ground, without getting lost in all of the features and capability built into the Enterprise edition.

SharePoint Server 2010 for Internet Sites, Enterprise

The Enterprise edition is intended for organizations looking to create customer-facing public Internet sites and private extranets using the full enterprise capabilities of SharePoint. As with the core Enterprise edition, the FIS Enterprise edition adds Access, Excel, InfoPath, PerformancePoint, and Visio services to the existing feature lineup.

Microsoft Office 365

Office 365 is a Microsoft's newest cloud offering, which combines the Microsoft Office desktop suite with online versions of SharePoint, Exchange, and Lync. Available in two plans, one for small business and one for midsize/enterprises, Office 365 offers users a feature-rich collaborative environment. With a simplified deployment, and security, reliability, and management being offloaded to the cloud provider, IT departments and business users can focus on other items, while knowing that the software infrastructure is being taken care of.

FAST Search Server 2010 for Internet Sites

As FAST Search Server 2010 is meant to be used with the SharePoint 2010 Enterprise edition, this version of FAST Server is meant to be used in conjunction with the FIS version for Internet websites.

Q: Where should I deploy SharePoint? What choices do I really have?

A: Now that you've decided what edition of SharePoint you want to make available to your company, your next step is to determine where your SharePoint environment is actually going to reside. This is no trivial decision as it will ultimately dictate the accessibility, usability, and administration of your environment. Your decision will also largely be driven by budgetary constraints, as each option has its own direct and indirect costs. As many organizations have realized, SharePoint tends to become a mission-critical application, so it would be a good idea for you to anticipate this from the get-go. To streamline your thought process, you should begin by asking yourself the following questions:

- Do I have existing technologies that I want to integrate?
- Do I have an existing infrastructure that I can leverage?
- Do I have the in-house staff to deploy and administer my environment?

- Am I planning on heavily customizing the environment, or will native functionality be adequate for my needs?

- Are there security or regulatory constraints that I should be concerned with?

- Do I want to be responsible for providing and adhering to basic Service Level Agreements, or do I want this outsourced?

- What degree of control do I need to maintain over the hardware, software, and so on, in my environment?

Perhaps the most basic and yet most important question of all is "Do you want to become an expert in SharePoint deployment, administration, and support, or do you want to rely on SharePoint experts to do it for you?"

All complexities and nuances aside, there are basically four general deployment roadmaps that you will need to choose between:

- On-premise
- Hosted
- Cloud
- Hybrid

On-premise

An on-premise or in-house deployment gives you the most flexibility and control over what you are going to make available to your user base. This is the traditional, most familiar deployment model, and every organization has gone through it in some variation. There are many benefits to an on-premise SharePoint 2010 deployment.

- **Control**: Your organization will have complete control over all hardware, software, and infrastructure decisions.

- **Patch management**: Since you own the infrastructure, all upgrades, updates, and changes can be performed and monitored at your discretion.

- **Application integration**: Additional Microsoft and non-Microsoft technology owned by your firm can be integrated with SharePoint at your leisure. This includes Exchange, Lync, Project Server, System Center Suite, SAP, Documentum, and so on.

- **Customization**: There is no limit to the customization of your SharePoint environment. You are free to develop and deploy as you and your developers please (with the appropriate change management policies in place, of course!).

- **On-site support and custom SLAs**: Since you own your IT staff and support teams, you can mutually set expectations with your end users and guarantee adherence to SLAs without compromise or outside interference.

However, as enticing as an in-house deployment may appear, there are some disadvantages that you need to consider:

- **Upfront and unpredictable costs**: A significant expenditure will be required for hardware, software, licensing, and potentially the hiring/training of IT staff members.

- **Reliability**: Your SharePoint environment will only be as reliable as the server closet, server room, or corporate datacenter it is located in. Ultimately, it can only be as good as the human and capital investment your company is willing to put into the infrastructure.

- **Performance and scalability**: If the environment is or becomes susceptible to seasonal traffic spikes and other inconsistent traffic patterns, it can be costly and difficult to scale the infrastructure and guarantee expected performance.

- **Support**: Most firms have a limited budget for IT staff, inherently a cost center, and will simply cumulatively try to add this responsibility to existing staff members. This may prove to be too complex a responsibility, and could impact staff performance, who may already be stretched thin supporting existing technologies.

 Supporting an enterprise SharePoint environment can require a significant investment in resources including hiring SharePoint administrators, database administrators, application developers, help-desk staff, and so on. Another common misconception is that SharePoint will seamlessly fit into the existing technical skill sets of current staff. This is usually not the case, due to the breadth and depth of the platform, the learning curve, and their already-limited bandwidth.

Hosted

Hosting your SharePoint 2010 deployment with a third-party provider, particularly one specializing in SharePoint hosting, may give you the performance and reliability that you are looking for. Inherently, a hosting provider's infrastructure can deliver the scalability, reliability, security, and regulatory environment that would be cost-prohibitive for an in-house deployment (naturally, these services come with their own price tags).

Additionally, since a SharePoint hosting provider likely assumes most managed services and support, this will free up your IT staff to focus on your business, rather than additional monitoring, maintenance, and administration. Some advantages of third-party hosting include:

- **Costs**: Hosting costs have become a predictable, operational expense. You know what you are paying for, and there shouldn't be any surprises.

- **Complex deployments**: Most hosting providers will be capable of configuring and integrating highly complex SharePoint implementations. Do your research. Talk to a few providers and determine to what degree you want to manage this implementation or have it be managed by someone else.

- **Disaster recovery and reliability**: Hosting providers are backed up and secured in disaster-resistant data centers; these service are being offered to you via pre-packaged plans, bundles, and contracts. This relieves the extra overhead and responsibility of you having to manually research, determine, purchase, renew, and so on. Review the service offerings and all SLA details before committing to a particular provider.

- **Regulatory compliance**: Many hosting providers have compliance certifications including Sarbanes-Oxley, HIPAA, and so on.

- **Scalability**: Traffic surges and spikes can be more easily accommodated.

- **Specialized staff**: Hosting providers employ highly trained specialists that will integrate with your team and assist you in every step of your deployment.

All of this may sound great, but you should still remember the following drawbacks:

- **Flexibility**: Although it comes close, third-party hosted will not recreate the level of flexibility that you will inherently have with an in-house deployment.

- **Portability**: Note that your organization will be contractually committed to your hosting provider. Switching providers, migrating the environment to the cloud, or migrating it back in-house can easily become a daunting task if you choose to opt out of your contract.

- **Change management and control**: Due diligence and advanced planning will be required, as most providers may have a formal review and approval process.

Cloud

Cloud computing has the ability to provide customers with minimal-effort, on-demand shared pool provisioning of computing resources to provide SharePoint 2010 availability. This approach manifests itself differently in all three general cloud offerings:

- **Infrastructure as a Service (IaaS)**: Infrastructure as a Service offers computing power, storage, and networking infrastructure as a service via the public Internet. SharePoint 2010 fits into this space by allowing you to launch the underlying infrastructure in public or private clouds. SharePoint 2010 is deployed on this infrastructure, which you ultimately own. This option gives you the most control and flexibility in terms of the cloud variants.

- **Software as a Service (SaaS)**: With Software as a Service, an entire application can be made available on demand. The application exists in the cloud and can be consumed from any browser. Microsoft's SaaS SharePoint offering is Office 365, which combines the Microsoft Office desktop suite with online versions of Exchange Online, SharePoint Online, and Microsoft Lync Online. This option is attractive to organizations where customization is of little importance, but it has a limited feature set and is inflexible in comparison to its on-premise, third-party hosted, or IaaS counterparts.

- **Platform as a Service (PaaS)**: A Platform as a Service environment offers a runtime environment for application code. This means that an entire virtual machine does not need to be built and configured; only the application code needs to be uploaded and started. In this model most of the infrastructure is owned by the customer, where only the portion running in the cloud adheres to that offering's binding SLAs. SharePoint 2010 provides many ways to integrate with the Azure Services Platform, Microsoft's PaaS offering. From simple SQL Azure data-centric applications, to complex workflow that leverages custom Azure services, there is much potential in integrating these two evolving technologies.

The following figure shows sample third-party hosting and cloud providers:

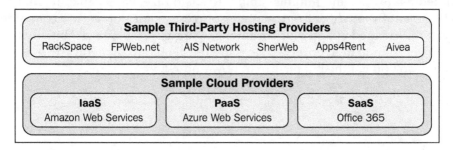

Hybrid

A hybrid deployment effectively combines an on-premise environment with a third-party hosting provider, with a virtual private cloud, or a combination of all three. There are also hybrid clouds, which blend public and private clouds to provide the benefits of both models. This deployment can also be perceived as one of the most common, especially for companies that are just starting to explore the cloud space. Companies will continue to use their existing on-premise infrastructure, but new software purchases and deployments are initiated in hosting facilities or in virtual private clouds. Obviously the endgame for most is to eventually move on-premise equipment elsewhere.

> The authors want to point out that the hybrid approach can be rather costly, since your organization would potentially be absorbing licensing and support costs for both the on-premise and hosted environments.

So what do I choose?

When it comes to SharePoint, there is no "one size fits all" solution. You have to carefully weigh the good with the bad, and correlate this against the expected user experience, and ultimately your budget. It is exactly the aim of this chapter to help you do this. If your company has a big budget, expects complete control and heavy customization, and has an IT team with the technical expertise and bandwidth to deploy and support SharePoint, then an on-premise solution might be a good fit. If you're willing to outsource the work to experts as an operational cost, but still expect some customization and on-demand control, then hosting might be a better option.

The same applies for all of the cloud offerings. IaaS will offer you the most flexibility and control, but also the most complexity in terms of implementation and ongoing support and maintenance. SaaS will provide a turn-key configuration, predictable costs, and a standardized user experience. This, however, comes at the compromise of a limited feature set and minimal ability to customize. PaaS will only offer you an environment from which to consume resources, so it is not really a contender in terms of a full-fledged SharePoint deployment strategy. It could potentially integrate with your solution to deliver the services in your final deployment, and is worth mentioning so you get the big picture of how and where it fits in.

Q: What about licensing? What are my options and how much will it cost?

A: Microsoft is notorious for having some of the most complicated licensing practices around. So much so that Microsoft even offers exams and certifications regarding licensing for small businesses or large organizations (`https://partner.microsoft.com/40029101`). Licensing options can also change, so please refer to the Microsoft Licensing website for the latest information. The two general Microsoft licensing constructs that you will be dealing with are **Server Licenses** and **Client Access Licenses (CALs)**. CALs can be further broken down into two types: **User CALs** and **Device CALs**.

Licensing SharePoint 2010 can be rather complex, so it is important to get a handle on this quickly. To get started, you will need to know the answers to the following questions:

- Which edition of SharePoint does my company need?
- Who are my end users?
- How many servers will actually run SharePoint?
- How many people or devices will access SharePoint?
- Is my company licensed for the Microsoft products that are needed to run SharePoint?

What edition of SharePoint does my company need?

As you learned in the previous section, SharePoint 2010 has three core editions, and each has a set of corresponding licenses.

- SharePoint Foundation 2010
    - Free download
    - Companies must be properly licensed for Microsoft Windows Server
- SharePoint Server 2010 Standard
    - Purchase SharePoint Server 2010
    - License the Standard feature set through Standard CALs (either User or Device CALs)

- SharePoint Server 2010 Enterprise

  ° Purchase SharePoint Server 2010

  ° License the Standard feature set through Standard CALs (either User or Device CALs)

  ° License the Enterprise feature set through Enterprise CALs (either User or Device CALs)

Who are my end users?

Is my company going to provide access to internal users (employees), external users (suppliers, customers, vendors, and the public), or both?

For internal users, SharePoint uses the **Server plus CAL** licensing model. This model requires the purchase of a server license for each server running the software, and User or Device CALs for the corresponding numbers of internal users. For the Standard edition, a Standard CAL will be required. For the Enterprise edition, a Standard CAL and an Enterprise CAL will be needed (Standard and Enterprise CALs are both required because CALs are considered cumulative). Note that this model can also be used for external users, but only if the external users are countable and CALs can be assigned to specific individuals.

For external users, SharePoint uses the **Server** licensing model. This model is intended for SharePoint Server 2010 Standard FIS and Enterprise FIS editions. Since no CALs are used in conjunction with this license, the server license is significantly more expensive than its on-premise counterpart. As with the previous licensing model, each server running the software will require its own server license.

 If you are planning on implementing a production SharePoint Internet site and a production SharePoint intranet, you will need to have the appropriate licenses for both. Please refer to the SharePoint licensing site (`http://sharepoint.microsoft.com/en-us/buy/pages/licensing-details.aspx`) for more details.

How many servers will run SharePoint?

Each running instance of the server software requires an individual server license (SharePoint Server 2010 or SharePoint Server 2010 for Internet Sites).

When using SharePoint Server 2010 for Internet sites to license external-facing scenarios, you need a license on all servers that will be used for external content, regardless of farm configuration or if users are directly accessing the server (staging, application, frontend, or index). The only exceptions are servers in a development/ test environment; these are typically covered by **MSDN (Microsoft Developer Network)** licensing.

> There might be scenarios where both internal and external users need to be supported on the same hardware. In this case, both types of server licenses can be assigned to the same servers and use the same running software instances.

How many people or devices will access SharePoint?

Microsoft offers two options when purchasing CALs:

- A device-based CAL (Device CAL)
- A user-based CAL (User CAL)

With a Device CAL, a CAL is required for every device that accesses a SharePoint 2010 Server, regardless of the number of people who use that device. With a User CAL, a CAL is required for every person who accesses a SharePoint 2010 Server, regardless of the number of devices used.

> You can choose the option that makes the most sense for your company's needs. For example, User CALs are well suited for employees who need roaming access using multiple devices, while Device CALs are a better fit for multiple shift workers who share devices.

Is my company licensed for the Microsoft products that are needed to run SharePoint?

SharePoint Server 2010 requires Microsoft Windows Server and Microsoft SQL Server; these licenses are not automatically included. Be sure you have the correct licenses for both Windows Server and SQL Server when working out your licensing strategy.

- Windows Server usually is licensed through the Server/CAL model
- A default installation of SharePoint Foundation will use SQL Server 2008 Express edition, which is free and does not tax you any licenses
- SQL Server has two primary licensing models, Server/CAL and per processor
- If you are planning on deploying and integrating other Microsoft products such as Project Server 2010, System Center Data Protection Manager 2010, ForeFront for SharePoint, and so on, remember that they have their own licenses and licensing requirements

Enterprise Agreement

The **Microsoft Enterprise Agreement (EA)** is a good option for your organization if you have more than 250 PCs, devices and/or users and want to license software and cloud services for your organization for a minimum three-year period. The EA is the best licensing program for organizations that want to standardize IT across the enterprise, yet retain the flexibility to choose from on-premises and cloud services.

With an EA, you'll get:

- Volume pricing with flexible payment options
- Full benefits of Software Assurance
- Flexibility to transition to cloud services at your own pace
- Simplified license management though a single, company-wide agreement
- Flexible, cost-effective, manageable licensing

Q: SharePoint 2010 Development, Quality Assurance, Production—how many farms do I actually need?

A: You know this concept inside out, but the complexity of multiple fully functional and integrated SharePoint farms might seem a bit daunting and, well frankly, expensive. Nonetheless, you need to consider multiple SharePoint farms simply because industry best practices and proper governance dictate separate **development** (DEV), **quality assurance** (QA) or **user acceptance testing** (UAT), and **production** (PROD) environments. Don't just think about customizations and Line Of Business applications; service packs and hotfixes must also go through a structured testing process, or you recklessly run the risk of corrupting your production environment and forcing an outage upon your end users.

 Disaster recovery (DR) farms are not mentioned in this section. SharePoint DR is a vast topic, with myriads of potential implementations. For information on SharePoint DR, refer to `http://technet.microsoft.com/en-us/sharepoint/ff601831`.

Smaller organizations can get away with just DEV and PROD, custom development performed locally or on a single dedicated server followed by controlled deployments to the production system. Large organizations will vary in terms of their change-control process, and the number of environments new code, applications, and patches will traverse before being released to the general public. In any case, you need to weigh industry best practices against what you can afford to do, and against what your organization's IT staff can support. It's basically risk versus reward. Consider the following concepts when making your decision:

- **Costs**: You will have to face the costs of running additional hardware to support multiple farms. Costs can be minimized by reducing your hardware footprint through virtualization or using cloud-based resources for development.

- **Licensing**: Luckily, Microsoft licensing won't be too much of an issue. Other than PROD, everything else should be covered using **Microsoft Developer Network (MSDN)** licenses. Make sure you have an MSDN subscription.

- **Consistency**: At the very least, the environments you put up should match in terms of operating system version, software versions, and patch levels. They should actually try to match the same hardware and configurations, and be integrated with the same backend systems, or acceptable clones of said systems. Infrastructure modifications must be reflected in all three environments to maintain consistent application and patch deployment governance.

- **Footprint**: Although consistency is required, the actual scale need not be the same. A development environment can be minimal; a single server or even multiple single servers assigned to individual developers (often seen when using the cloud for development). A quality assurance environment will have a bigger footprint than DEV, but is not responsible for economies of scale like PROD. Nonetheless, it should mimic a minimized architectural representation of its bigger brother, so that testing there is representative of and predicts the ultimate end user experience in PROD.

- **Independence**: The environments should be logically and physically separate. In a perfect world this means hardware separation, network separation, Active Directory Domain Services separation, and so on. Actions in one environment should not have any influence on actions in any of the other environments.

- **Governance**: Multiple environments will assist in properly formalizing standards, procedures, and policies. This includes setting testing and validation standards, approving and regulating acceptable maintenance practices, establishing and ratifying packing and installation methods, and so on.

- **Support**: Having multiple environments will require additional IT support, another direct and indirect cost. But you still need to consider the alternative, a capital investment that goes to waste because of a lack of structured change control policies, ultimately resulting in an unstable, unreliable, and unadoptable system.

The following figure shows simplified, sample architectures for the DEV, QA/UAT, and PROD farms of an enterprise SharePoint environment, with respect to scale and hardware footprint. The development environment illustrates a single server hosting all of the SharePoint roles, protected/accessed via a standard firewall/proxy server (consider Microsoft Forefront TMG or UAG 2010 mentioned later on in this chapter, designed for use with SharePoint 2010). In the quality assurance farm, the SharePoint roles are segregated into tiers (web, application, and database). This is a minimum footprint model of the full-scale production farm, mimicking the production architecture to simulate a valid end user experience for testers and QA engineers. The production farm is designed for capacity, high performance, and availability, with groups of servers allocated for the specific roles.

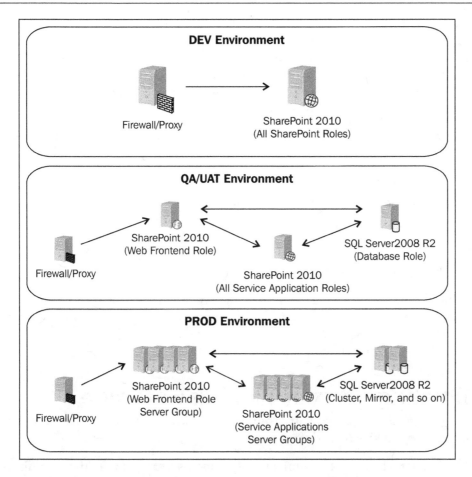

Q: What do I need to know about storage requirements and their impact on my deployment strategy?

A: You have documents stored everywhere, don't you? File servers, network attached storage, storage area networks (SANs) — these are some of the storage devices that maintain the whole document corpus of your organization. But what happens to all of these documents when you make the eventual move to SharePoint? End users will definitely want to use the Enterprise Search capability of SharePoint to find documents, regardless of where they are located in the enterprise. You are also going to move a good portion of documents and records into SharePoint (it is an enterprise content management system after all).

While it is the duty of your IT department to sort out the technical specifics, you should understand the basics of SharePoint capacity planning, especially in terms of storage. This will give you a better idea of what storage is going to cost you. Each of the deployment types (on-premise, hosted, cloud-based) will have different costs associated with how storage is procured and used, so we'd recommend you know what you are in for before deciding on a strategy.

Several SharePoint architectural factors will influence your storage needs and your design, including:

- The amount of content
- Deployed features and service applications
- The number of farms
- Availability needs
- Throughput and latency targets

Since SharePoint is database-driven, the majority of data is probably going to be stored in content databases and databases used by service applications, so database sizing, data architecture, and database server hardware are all very important considerations towards creating an optimal solution.

Estimating content database storage

To help get you started, Microsoft provides the following simplistic formula to estimate the rough size of a content database:

1. Calculate the expected number of documents (referred to in the formula as D).
2. Estimate the average size of the documents that you will be storing (referred to in the formula as S).
3. Estimate the number of list items in the environment (referred to in the formula as L).
4. Determine the approximate number of versions (referred to in the formula as V).

 Use the following formula to estimate the size of your content databases: *Content Database size = $((D \times V) \times S) + (10\ KB \times (L + (V \times D)))$*.

The value of 10 KB in the formula is a constant that roughly estimates the amount of metadata required by SharePoint Server 2010; obviously this would be increased if your deployment required significant use of metadata.

Please note that this formula is just a starting point, and by no means comprehensive in terms of your total storage needs. Even with content databases, there are additional factors that affect the size including recycle bins, auditing and auditing data, Office web apps, the Office web apps cache, and so on.

Data scale

This is perhaps your greatest concern. Data scale represents the volume of data your server farms can store while still meeting latency and throughput goals. The greater the amount of data, the greater the impact on the overall throughput and end user experience. The methods used to transfer data across disks and database servers can also affect latency and throughput.

Some examples of optimizing a farm for data and storage performance include the following:

- Sufficient database server resources
- Proper database distribution across database servers
- Proper database volume distribution (for example using unique **Logical Units (LUNs)**, consisting of unique physical disk spindles in SAN configurations)
- Use of **Remote BLOB Storage (RBS)** to store **Binary Large Objects (BLOBs)** data on less expensive storage devices

Q: Intranet, extranet—which SharePoint topology is right for me?

A: Good question; unfortunately only you can answer that. SharePoint topologies can be very simple (a single-server intranet) or can become incredibly complex (a global, multi-lingual extranet with cross-farm services). Your business should understand the requirements and goals clearly and very early on in the planning phases, before financially committing yourself to any particular design. Ask yourself the following questions:

- Who are my target end users?
- What type of content am I exposing?
- What is my budget?

- What will it cost me to plan ahead and do the work now, rather than risk re-architecting later?

- Would this topology be more optimal on-premise, hosted, or in the cloud?

Intranets

A SharePoint 2010 intranet environment is the classic web application—a private network that can only be physically accessed within your organization. This is the cheapest and simplest topology that an organization would choose. It is simple in terms of licensing, configuration, overhead, and manageability. Besides internal employees, it is also suitable for firms that have small numbers of external users who can be accounted for through the current licensing model, and serviced via existing access methods (such as via VPN). This topology should not require a complicated networking infrastructure, nor should you have to invest in additional supporting technologies to provide immediate value to end users.

Extranets

An extranet environment is a private network that is securely extended to share part of an organization's information or processes with external users such as partners, vendors, and clients. Extranets are used to share information and to offer alternatives for employees to work from remote locations. However, properly setting up an extranet requires outlining specific business requirements and giving important consideration to the following items:

- **Networking and hardware infrastructure**: Your requirements will dictate the changes and additions to your IT infrastructure, so be prepared to invest in hardware, software, and networking equipment.

- **Disparate identity management systems and access**: External users will likely be members of independent identity stores. This will impact how accounts will be managed and how other systems will interface with your environment.

- **Security and isolation**: Content will need to be isolated and segmented, based on the access rights of external users and their parent organizations. This will require significant planning and oversight, especially if your organization is bound by regulatory compliance.

Many formal SharePoint 2010 extranet topologies exist, but they are outside the scope of this book. Just to give you an idea, these include configurations such as the Edge Firewall, back-to-back perimeter, back-to-back with cross-farm services, and Split back-to-back. You can find more information on these and other topologies in the *Digging deeper* section at the end of this chapter.

Public-facing Internet sites

Many organizations have built their public Internet presence using SharePoint 2010. If you are thinking about going down this road, note the following considerations:

- **Licensing**: As mentioned earlier, specific licenses are required for this type of setup

- **Access**: Determine the purpose of your site and access requirements, external authenticated users versus anonymous users

- **Functionality**: There are specific caveats for anonymous users when it comes to workflows, forms, and other features

Some sample Fortune 500 companies that have public sites powered by SharePoint 2010 include Kraft Foods, HESS, Bristol-Meyers Squibb, Phillip Morris International, and DELL (financial services).

Q: What about authentication for end users; what options are available to me?

A: Your SharePoint 2010 deployment can manifest itself as an intranet, an extranet, a public-facing Internet site, or any permutation of these. Each of these topologies has its own constraints when it comes to access for internal or external users. Luckily for us, SharePoint 2010 comes with a myriad of built-in and extensible authentication options, which will give you the tools you need to set up your intended environment and end user experience. You can also use multiple authentication mechanisms against the same web applications, giving you further flexibility with site exposure and access. When planning an authentication strategy for your SharePoint environment, review the nuances and trade-offs of the available authentication types. Pay particular attention to security, browser compatibility, and difficulty in configuration.

Authentication in SharePoint 2010 has been consolidated into two categories, **Classic** and **Claims-Based** (please refer to the following figure for a breakdown). The specific authentication methods available through SharePoint 2010 are:

- **Windows**: NTLM, Kerberos, Anonymous, Basic, Digest

- **Forms-based**: **Lightweight Directory Access Protocol (LDAP)**, Microsoft SQL Server database or other database, custom or third-party membership and role providers

- **SAML token-based**: **Active Directory Federation Services (AD FS) 2.0**, third-party identity provider, Lightweight Directory Access Protocol (LDAP)

The following figure shows the different authentication mechanisms available in SharePoint 2010, and what categories they fall under.

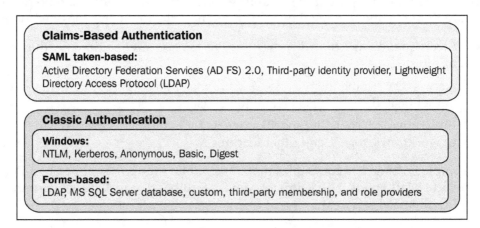

SharePoint itself does not actually authenticate users. SharePoint provides the platform where users are authenticated against providers (most commonly against Active Directory or an LDAP store).

 New to SharePoint 2010, **Claims-Based Authentication** is now the foundation on which all other authentication is built. All previous authentication methods from SharePoint 2007 are still available.

Funny you should say that...

This section of the chapter aims to address some common questions and concerns, typically voiced during a SharePoint deployment.

Q: Is there any way for me to migrate my existing licenses, instead of having to obtain new ones?

A: As of matter of fact, now there is! Previously, customers had no way of transferring licenses between on-premise and hosted environments. However, as of July 1, 2011, on-premise licenses can easily be transferred directly to a hosting provider, or to the cloud (for example to an Amazon Web Services instance). This is known as **License Mobility through Microsoft Software Assurance**.

License Mobility through Microsoft Software Assurance gives Microsoft Volume Licensing customers with active Microsoft Software Assurance the flexibility to deploy Windows server applications where they please. With the Software Assurance benefit, customers do not need to purchase new licenses, and there are no associated mobility fees. This license mobility currently covers Microsoft SharePoint Server, and also SQL Server, Exchange Server, Lync Server, System Center servers, and Dynamics CRM.

 As always when it comes to licensing, be sure to get proper help from an authorized license mobility partner.

Q: What do I need to know about web browsers, tablets, and mobile phones?

A: The following sections describe web browsers, mobile phones, and tablets:

Web browsers

SharePoint 2010 supports several commonly used web browsers. However, certain web browsers might cause some SharePoint Server 2010 functionality to be downgraded, limited, or available only through alternative steps. In some cases, certain functionality might not even be available at all. Review the browsers used in your organization to ensure they will provide the end user experience you are anticipating. Microsoft divides browser support into the following levels:

- **Supported**: All features and functionality work. If you encounter any issues, support can help you to resolve these issues. Browsers: Internet Explorer (IE) 9 (32-bit), IE 8 (32-bit), IE 7 (32-bit).

- **Supported with known limitations**: Most features work, but if some do not or are disabled by design, documentation on how to resolve these issues is readily available. Browsers: Internet Explorer (IE) 9 (64-bit), IE 8 (64-bit), IE 7 (64-bit), Mozilla Firefox 3.6, Safari 4.04.

- **Not tested**: This means that compatibility has not been tested and you are likely to run into issues. Browser: IE 6 (32-bit).

- **Not supported**: Web browsers that are not listed in the previous categories are not supported. Sample browsers: Internet Explorer 5.01, Internet Explorer 5.5x, Internet Explorer for Macintosh, and earlier versions of third-party web browsers listed previously.

For a full list of supported browsers, please see http://technet.microsoft.com/en-us/library/cc263526.aspx.

Mobile phones

SharePoint 2010 includes support for using mobile phones to access documents, lists, and calendars, perform people and document searches, and receive SMS alerts on content. With Microsoft SharePoint Workspace Mobile 2010, users can use Windows Phones to access offline documents on SharePoint 2010. iPhone users can use SharePlus, Apple's client application for SharePoint (`http://itunes.apple.com/gb/app/shareplus-office-mobile-client/id364895421?mt=8`). Android users can use SP Elements (`http://www.spelements.com/android/`).

A variety of mobile browsers are supported, including:

- IE Mobile on Windows Mobile 5/6 and newer versions
- Safari 4 and newer versions on the iPhone (3/4) and iPad (1/2)
- BlackBerry 4.x and newer versions
- NetFront 3.4, 3.5 and newer versions
- Opera Mobile 8.65 and newer versions

Tablets

Tablets present a new way for users to interact with your environment. The tablet market is growing rapidly, and SharePoint 2010 does provide an effective end user experience. Users can access SharePoint content using the mobile browsers provided by their tablets, or by purchasing SharePoint-centric apps such as **SharePlus, DocumentsToGo, Mobile Entrée**, and so on. Now is the time to evaluate how tablets will work within your corporate SharePoint environment to stay ahead of the curve!

Q: Why are companies resistant to My Sites; can this attitude ever change?

A: SharePoint's **My Sites** are personal sites that give users a central location to manage and store their links, documents, and contacts. Although companies may also have business-specific reasons for choosing not to deploy My Sites, the two main anti-drivers are the following:

- They don't see the value in it, or see it as a distraction
- The lack of control over what users post scares them

The value of My Sites is not immediately apparent or easily measurable. Many organizations are entrenched with process-based work and metric-based performance measurement. The move towards tacit knowledge, and how tacit knowledge influences decision and profitability is very difficult to measure, and therefore justify.

Traditional organizations restrict the activities and exposure of their employees. With My Sites, these same organizations are effectively distributing control to these employees and giving them a voice across the enterprise. This is a scary and novel concept to many organizations, who have not yet embraced the slow move towards social networking within an organization.

People are already used to social media and social networking, and it is only a matter of time before Enterprise 2.0 concepts become a standard part of organizations. As organizations bring on new talent and look to provide improved collaboration, they will first want to leverage what they already have, and this means activating the Enterprise 2.0 features available through SharePoint.

Q: I've heard that Office 2010 is the only version that integrates with SharePoint 2010. Is this true, and what are some other MS products that integrate with SharePoint 2010?

A: Here's the bottom line: to achieve the best end user experience with Microsoft Office and SharePoint integration, upgrade your client software to Microsoft Office Professional Plus 2010. You can use Office 2003, or Office 2007, but these versions will not have as complete integration as Office 2010 does. Obviously, Office 2003 will have the weakest performance of the bunch.

SharePoint is positioned as the tent pole for any organization, and most Microsoft software is built with the intention of integrating with SharePoint. The following is a list of premier Microsoft products that you might be interested in as part of your deployment roadmap:

Disaster recovery

This subject is often viewed as the most important aspect of SharePoint. **MS System Center Data Protection Manager** is part of the System Center family of management products from Microsoft and delivers unified data protection for SQL Server, Exchange, SharePoint, and so on.

Antivirus

MS Forefront Protection 2010 for SharePoint is a product that helps protect Microsoft Office SharePoint Server 2010 deployments from viruses, unwanted files, and inappropriate content.

Security

MS Forefront Threat Management Gateway 2010 (TMG) is a secure web gateway that provides comprehensive protection against web-based threats by integrating multiple layers of protections into a unified, easy-to-use solution.

MS Forefront Unified Access Gateway 2010 (UAG) delivers comprehensive, secure remote access to corporate resources for employees, partners, and vendors on both managed and unmanaged PCs and mobile devices.

Monitoring and management

System Center Operations Manager is a series of management packs for SharePoint 2010 that enables operators and administrators to manage Microsoft SharePoint 2010 products including SharePoint Server 2010, Project Server 2010, Search Server 2010, and Office Web Apps.

Project management

MS Project Server is a web-based project management software suit, built on SharePoint Server 2010. This software provides innovative capabilities across the entire lifecycle to help organizations effectively initiate, select, plan, and deliver projects on time and within budget.

Business intelligence

Duet Enterprise for Microsoft SharePoint and SAP extends the SAP product functionality to SharePoint. It provides complete flexibility and extensibility to compose solutions that blend the worlds of process and collaboration.

HP Business Decision Appliance is a self-service business intelligence appliance, optimized for SQL Server 2008 R2 and SharePoint Server 2010.

Client applications

Microsoft SharePoint Workspace 2010 expands the boundaries of collaboration by allowing fast, anytime, anywhere access to your Microsoft SharePoint team sites. Synchronize SharePoint Server 2010 document libraries with SharePoint Workspace so you can access, view, and edit files anytime and anywhere from your computer.

SharePoint Designer 2010 a free tool by Microsoft that allows users and developers alike to quickly create SharePoint solutions and respond to business needs.

Digging deeper

This chapter introduced the reader to deployment strategies for SharePoint. The following section provides references to sources of deployment information that the reader should reference to further understand deployment strategies for SharePoint 2010.

SharePoint editions

- Compare SharePoint Editions: http://sharepoint.microsoft.com/en-us/buy/Pages/Editions-Comparison.aspx
- SharePoint 2010 Editions Comparison Matrix: http://sharepoint-sandbox.com/index.php?/SharePoint-2010/General-Information/sp2010-sharepoint-2010-editions-comparison-matrix.html
- SharePoint 2010 Search: http://sharepoint.microsoft.com/en-us/product/capabilities/search/Pages/Search-Server.aspx
- Microsoft Case Study | General Mills: http://www.microsoft.com/casestudies/Microsoft-FAST-Search-Server-2010-For-Sharepoint/General-Mills/General-Mills-Frees-More-Time-for-Innovation-with-Research-Focused-Search-Application/4000007255

SharePoint licensing

- Licensing Details—SharePoint: http://sharepoint.microsoft.com/en-us/buy/pages/licensing-details.aspx
- SQL Server Licensing: http://www.microsoft.com/sqlserver/2008/en/us/licensing.aspx

- Window Server 2008 R2 Licensing: `http://www.microsoft.com/windowsserver2008/en/us/licensing-R2.aspx`
- Enterprise Agreement: `http://www.microsoft.com/licensing/licensing-options/enterprise.aspx`

Capacity planning

- Capacity Planning and Sizing Overview: `http://technet.microsoft.com/en-us/library/ff758647.aspx`
- Storage and SQL Server Capacity Planning: `http://technet.microsoft.com/en-us/library/cc298801.aspx`
- Plan for RBS: `http://technet.microsoft.com/en-us/library/ff628583.aspx`
- What's New In SharePoint 2010 Capacity Planning: `http://www.sharepointjoel.com/Lists/Posts/Post.aspx?ID=332`

Extranet topologies

- Best Practice for Extranet Environments: `http://technet.microsoft.com/en-us/library/hh204611.aspx`
- SharePoint 2010: Outlining Common Extranet Scenarios & Topologies; `http://programming4.us/enterprise/3136.aspx`

Public-facing SharePoint sites

- Fortune 500 Companies Using SharePoint: `http://www.topsharepoint.com/fortune-500-companies-using-sharepoint`

Authentication mechanisms

- Plan Authentication Methods: `http://technet.microsoft.com/en-us/library/cc262350.aspx`
- Plan Browser Support: `http://technet.microsoft.com/en-us/library/cc263526.aspx`

Summary

This chapter covered fundamental considerations for putting together your SharePoint deployment roadmap. You've learned about the different SharePoint editions, licensing requirements, where you can host or deploy your SharePoint farms, the different topologies available to you, planning for storage, authentication options, and potential hardware/software footprints for your deployments. You've also learned about SharePoint options for the mobile user, reviewed the adoption of Enterprise 2.0 capabilities, and explored other Microsoft technologies that interface with SharePoint.

We have covered a lot of ground, but only scratched the surface of each topic. The deep dive can be left to your IT teams. Nonetheless, by properly addressing all of the concepts in this chapter, you will be in a great place to lead the charge in your SharePoint deployment or migration. Of course, there will always be unspoken challenges and unanticipated hurdles, but you will come armed with a panoramic perspective. You have the knowledge; how you choose to utilize it is up to you.

While we briefly covered cloud concepts earlier, deploying SharePoint in the cloud is a topic that deserves its own chapter. As cloud computing becomes more ubiquitous, it is likely that you will start leaning towards this direction for most, if not all, of your future needs. The following chapter explores SharePoint deployments using Office 365 and the Amazon Web Services cloud.

4
SharePoint in the Clouds

The previous chapter outlined general decisions and concerns that need to be addressed when formalizing your SharePoint deployment roadmap. One of these decisions involves choosing a residence for your SharePoint environment(s): on-premise, hosted, in the cloud, and so on. As discussed earlier, each option clearly has its own set of benefits and disadvantages. However, to reiterate the general theme of these two chapters, *there is no one-size-fits-all implementation*. The deployment types are not mutually exclusive. Each set of requirements will be unique and, more than likely, you will find your organization creating a hybrid solution to exploit the benefits offered by the different deployment models.

To that end, the cloud can be your biggest catalyst and enabler. Whether you like it or not, the cloud has arrived, and it is something your organization should evaluate and consider. Cloud-based computing is transforming the information technology space and you need to understand what the cloud can do for SharePoint. As you learned in the previous chapter, all three cloud-computing models provide potential solutions for SharePoint. The Infrastructure as a Service (IaaS) model leverages virtualization, networking, and storage to build a managed infrastructure for SharePoint. The Platform as a Service (PaaS) model builds on top of this concept by guaranteeing the underlying infrastructure and allowing the organization only to focus on developing and consuming the SharePoint services that it needs, directly from the cloud. The Software as a Service (SaaS) model removes all administration and management responsibility from the organization. Your users simply sign on and use the services that you've approved for them.

But to effectively choose which cloud-computing models are optimal for your organization, you need to look deeper at the specific offerings, their respective costs, management overhead, typical uses, ownership of data, demarcation of responsibility, and so on. After all, there are many misconceptions about the cloud, which lead to incorrect assumptions. This chapter evaluates the available cloud offerings, with a focus on Office 365 for SaaS, Windows Azure for PaaS, and Amazon Web Services for IaaS.

> Please note that this is probably the most technical chapter in this handbook because it evaluates the available cloud offerings and aims to clear up any ambiguities about SharePoint and the cloud. If you're the kind of guy who isn't interested in "how it works", then this chapter is probably not for you.

By the time you finish reading this chapter, you should have enough insight and ammunition to start making confident, accurate decisions about SharePoint and cloud-based computing.

Q: What options do I actually have for cloud-based SharePoint 2010?

A: The IaaS, SaaS, and PaaS models are one way to group and view SharePoint offerings in the cloud. However, there is another dimension that you need to consider. This dimension is the *type of cloud* to be deployed. Each category has its own benefits and disadvantages, which should be carefully reviewed prior to making any architectural commitments.

There are four general cloud deployment models that can be considered for SharePoint:

- Public cloud
- Private cloud
- Community cloud
- Hybrid cloud

Public cloud

In a **public cloud** deployment, 100 percent of your SharePoint resources are hosted externally to your firm. This enables your organization to take advantage of increased reliability, stability, variable load, and disposable computing. SharePoint public cloud computing is available in SaaS, PaaS, and IaaS flavors, although only SaaS and IaaS offer the ability to host 100 percent of your resource pool. In terms of SaaS, Microsoft provides SharePoint cloud services through its **Office 365** program in the form of Standard and Dedicated SharePoint Online. This subscription-based offering is suitable and scalable to businesses of all sizes.

A PaaS offering provides the facilities to support the complete lifecycle of building and delivering web applications and services, without servers that you need to configure or administer. These facilities are provided entirely over the Internet, which can save your firm from the costs and complexities traditionally involved in buying and managing the underlying supporting hardware and software. To illustrate the PaaS model, **Windows Azure** integrates with SharePoint to service customers through common cloud applications and the extension of on-premise code. By extending on-premise code and applications into the Azure cloud, your organization can benefit from a greater pool of development resources, faster deployment times, and so on. Although a full SharePoint deployment cannot be hosted on Azure, it does provide a public computing cloud platform to scale and run SharePoint applications.

The IaaS model can be demonstrated with the **Amazon Elastic Compute Cloud (Amazon EC2)** public cloud. Amazon EC2 provides a managed infrastructure, but your organization is wholly responsible for deploying, maintaining, and administering your environment (as is the case with any IaaS provider). With Office 365 (SaaS) and Windows Azure (PaaS), the underlying infrastructures are guaranteed by SLAs and they are not exposed to you; your organization's only focus is on the services and applications. With Amazon EC2 (IaaS), although your entire infrastructure can be hosted externally, the management of that infrastructure is still your organization's responsibility.

Each public cloud model has its own sets of advantages and disadvantages. General disadvantages of SaaS include limited feature sets and less flexibility with regards to application customization, since you are typically dealing with services tailored to satisfy the needs of the masses, and a shared underlying infrastructure that you don't have access to. The upside in SaaS models is reduced cost of ownership and minimal administrative overhead.

With PaaS, you can support quick, agile implementations coupled with reducing the total cost of ownership, by paying for only the specific resources you need to develop, test, and deliver your applications. However, potential disadvantages include increased integration complexity and integration costs.

IaaS boasts a flexible, utility service model with a reduced total cost of ownership. But this only refers to the underlying infrastructure provided by the vendor. The actual customer environment built on this infrastructure still requires management, maintenance, fault-tolerance, business continuity, and so on, which are the customer's responsibility and will not offset personnel costs.

Private cloud

A **private cloud** exhibits many of the same concepts and services as a public cloud, but on-premise. It uses resources that are dedicated to your organization, but shares many of the characteristics of public cloud computing including resource pooling, elasticity, self-service, and rapid provisioning. In a private cloud, an organization controls the physical server infrastructure on which virtual servers reside. This allows an organization to share hardware costs, scale up or down on-demand, and to quickly recover from failures.

Private clouds can be managed on-premise, or hosted by a third-party cloud provider. On-premise private cloud solutions can be built using software stacks from Microsoft, VMWare, Eucalyptus, and so on. Using **Amazon Virtual Private Cloud (Amazon VPC)** as a third-party provider lets you provision a private, isolated section of the **Amazon Web Services (AWS)** cloud. There you can launch your SharePoint infrastructure into a virtual network topology that closely resembles the traditional network you would otherwise operate in your own datacenter.

In terms of features and customization, private clouds give you the most flexibility, since SharePoint is controlled internally. On-premise private clouds might even be considered the best functional option, due to the specialized nature of SharePoint. However, with a private cloud you cannot reduce up-front costs nor decrease administration and maintenance overhead. Implementing and administering a private cloud will require specialized technical skill sets and a dedicated team. You may be able to share costs by using your private cloud for many different systems, but high up-front investments won't be removed from the equation as with public cloud offerings. With that said, externally hosted private clouds are likely to be cheaper than their on-premise counterparts since your organization won't need to concern itself with immediate capital outlays, short hardware lifecycles, and as high a level of human resource investment.

Community cloud

A **community cloud** environment is characterized as a common infrastructure shared by many organizations with similar needs or common concerns. Community clouds do not offer the same cost savings as public clouds, because fewer users are sharing the infrastructure costs. But they are also less expensive than private clouds, since costs are distributed amongst multiple organizations. Community clouds can be functionally similar to private or public clouds, but membership is restricted to members of a specific community or vertical industry. They can be managed on-premise, but are more commonly handled by a third-party hosting provider, and can offer a range of services including IaaS, SaaS, or PaaS. Community clouds are ideal for government, non-profit, healthcare, and education sectors, since these institutions typically adhere to compliance regulations, and tend to have unique data privacy and security requirements. Some examples of community clouds include: Optum Health Cloud, for those in the healthcare industry to take advantage of cloud resources; IGT Cloud, a cloud aimed specifically at gaming companies; and Google Apps for Government. Microsoft is currently creating a government-only community cloud option for Office 365.

Hybrid cloud

A **hybrid cloud** is usually a combination of two or more clouds that remain unique entities, but are integrated together to offer the benefits of multiple deployment models. They can also consist of virtualized and physical infrastructures, as typically occurs when an organization transitions from an on-premise SharePoint deployment to a cloud offering. Hybrid clouds are often used by companies who want to utilize cloud computing, but are still concerned about security, and certain regulatory and compliance standards. They are typically managed by a third-party hosting provider, or created by integrating PaaS functionality to augment the offering.

The following figure highlights some of the general benefits and disadvantages of the different cloud computing models with respect to SharePoint 2010:

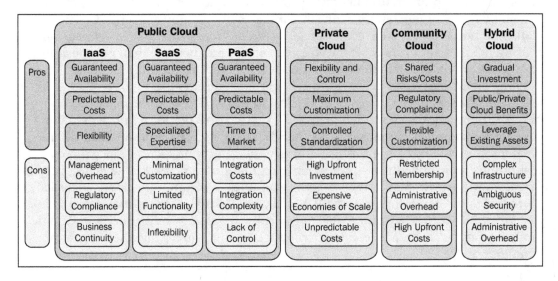

	Public Cloud			Private Cloud	Community Cloud	Hybrid Cloud
	IaaS	**SaaS**	**PaaS**			
Pros	Guaranteed Availability	Guaranteed Availability	Guaranteed Availability	Flexibility and Control	Shared Risks/Costs	Gradual Investment
	Predictable Costs	Predictable Costs	Predictable Costs	Maximum Customization	Regulatory Complaince	Public/Private Cloud Benefits
	Flexibility	Specialized Expertise	Time to Market	Controlled Standardization	Flexible Customization	Leverage Existing Assets
Cons	Management Overhead	Minimal Customization	Integration Costs	High Upfront Investment	Restricted Membership	Complex Infrastructure
	Regulatory Compliance	Limited Functionality	Integration Complexity	Expensive Economies of Scale	Administrative Overhead	Ambiguous Security
	Business Continuity	Inflexibility	Lack of Control	Unpredictable Costs	High Upfront Costs	Administrative Overhead

Q: How can I use Amazon Web Services for SharePoint 2010?

A: To get a grasp on this, let's take a look at the Amazon Web Services (AWS) platform and some of the specific offerings that are available and relevant to a SharePoint implementation. AWS is a collection of remote computing services that together create a cloud computing platform. This platform provides a myriad of products in various functional categories including computing, storage, messaging, content delivery, networking, and so on. But AWS is also characterized as a full IaaS provider, and it is this capability that we would be harnessing for a SharePoint infrastructure. The Amazon offerings that we would typically use include the following:

- Amazon Elastic Compute Cloud (Amazon EC2)
- Amazon Elastic Block Store (Amazon EBS)
- Amazon Virtual Private Cloud (Amazon VPC)
- Elastic Load Balancing (ELB)

This is not at all an exhaustive list, but it is a starting point for your cloud-based deployment roadmap. These products would essentially form the backbone for your SharePoint implementation and are described in more detail in the following sections.

Amazon Elastic Compute Cloud

Amazon EC2 is the core offering that provides your organization with resizable computing capacity in the Amazon cloud. EC2 is an elastic computing environment that provides you flexibility in terms of hardware configurations, operating systems, software packages, and so on. Through this service you can retain complete control over your computing resources while resting assured that your instances are safely running on and guaranteed by Amazon's computing infrastructure. Server provisioning may have once taken hours or days; your organization can now provision server instances in minutes.

So how do you leverage this for SharePoint? EC2 will be the backbone service that provides your SharePoint server infrastructure, allowing your organization to take advantage of all EC2 capabilities. This includes potentially doing the following:

- Creating template server images (called Amazon Machine Images or AMIs) for the different SharePoint roles, to reduce provisioning complexity and overhead
- Scaling individual SharePoint servers vertically by modifying hardware resources on the fly
- Scaling SharePoint servers horizontally by adding additional server instances for a particular SharePoint role or service application
- Creating redundancy and high availability architectures by distributing server instances between different availability zones within a region, between different national regions, different global regions, and so on

Amazon Elastic Block Store

Amazon EBS provides persistent storage for Amazon EC2 instances through block-level storage volumes. This off-instance storage persists independently from the lifetime of an instance. EBS volumes are highly available and highly reliable, and can be used for boot partitions and as standard storage volumes. For SharePoint, ways in which EBS can be used include the following:

- Creating EBS volumes for the different drives used by the SharePoint and SQL server instances
- Using EBS snapshots to backup SharePoint server instances, content, databases, and so on

Amazon Virtual Private Cloud

Amazon VPC allows your organization to provision a virtual private cloud on an isolated segment of Amazon's scalable infrastructure, where you can specify and control your own virtual networking topology. Amazon VPC can be used to create a completely independent network solely in the cloud, with public-facing subnets and multiple layers of security. Alternatively, Amazon VPC can be used to extend your on-premise network into the cloud, by creating connectivity between your corporate datacenters and your VPC. Whatever the specific requirement or strategy, Amazon VPC is very flexible and can adapt to virtually any scenario. Sample SharePoint deployments in VPCs include the following:

- A standalone SharePoint deployment hosted in a resource forest in a VPC

- A SharePoint deployment that is connected to and part of an on-premise domain, but hosted in a VPC

- A hybrid SharePoint deployment where some components are physically hosted in a datacenter, while others are deployed in a VPC

Elastic Load Balancing

ELB is a method of automatically distributing incoming application traffic across multiple Amazon EC2 server instances. With ELB, your organization can achieve fault tolerance in its applications via health detection, session affinity, security, elastic scaling, and so on. For SharePoint, ELB could be used to:

- Distribute load to role-based server instances in a SharePoint farm

- Create a redundant and highly-available SharePoint farm by distributing incoming traffic across a single Availability Zone or multiple Availability Zones

As mentioned earlier, Amazon provides a plethora of products and services. The ones mentioned previously will play an immediate part in the design and implementation of your cloud-based SharePoint infrastructure. However, there are additional products that might not have as direct an impact or might not be as obvious in your design. In any case, it is good for you to be aware of them, and how they could prove beneficial in your SharePoint architectural design. These include:

- **Auto Scaling**: This potentially integrates with ELB to automatically up or downscale your SharePoint capacity

- **Amazon CloudWatch**: This is a web service to provide monitoring of your Amazon EC2 SharePoint server instances

- **Amazon Route 53**: You can use Amazon's DNS web service to route end users to your organization's public SharePoint sites

- **Amazon Direct Connect**: This is used to establish a dedicated network connection from your on-premise network to AWS, creating a hybrid SharePoint infrastructure

Q: This doesn't sound like a turn-key solution. Where does Amazon's responsibility end and where does mine begin?

A: Turn-key solution? Definitely not! Any IaaS implementation inherently cannot be a turn-key solution, since it only accounts for management of the underlying infrastructure, and not the custom application environment built on top of it. What do we mean by the underlying infrastructure in terms of Amazon? This would include:

- The facilities that house the hardware

- The combined hardware on which the cloud is realized

- The intra- and inter-networking of these facilities

- Supported Amazon Machine Images (AMIs)

- Adherence to licensing for operating system and other general software

- Personnel required to ensure support, operation, and uptime of the AWS products and services as specified in the Amazon SLAs

Please note that Amazon provides AMIs that come pre-packaged with default Windows operating system installations. Windows licensing costs are bundled into the cost of using these specific AMIs. Amazon also provides AMIs pre-packaged with Windows and SQL; in these cases, Windows and SQL licensing are bundled into usage costs. However, this is the current extent to which Microsoft products come pre-packaged. Amazon only supports the default operation and condition of its AMIs; any customization/configuration is the customer's responsibility, as is any additional software installation and adherence to that software's licensing requirements (this means SharePoint).

Amazon provides your organization with the tools and the capacity to realize your vision. However, it is still your vision and it is up to you to realize it. Amazon does not manage your custom application infrastructure, and it is important for you to clearly understand this demarcation point.

As an aside, this is particularly important in terms of business continuity. Amazon provides general guidelines for highly available, redundant architectures, but does not enforce that you build them. It is up to your organization to do the appropriate amount of research, decide on an acceptable level of cost versus risk, and deploy in accordance with best practices. To reiterate, in an IaaS environment, most of the responsibility falls on your organization, so make sure you've exhaustively evaluated your proposed architecture. The success of your deployment heavily depends on adequate preparation, planning, and foresight.

In terms of a SharePoint deployment, you have to look at the architectural panorama. Understand all of the architectural pieces involved, how they need to integrate together, and what you have at your disposal to make this happen. Try to separate and envision your overall infrastructure in three layers:

- Amazon infrastructure
- Windows infrastructure
- SharePoint infrastructure

Amazon infrastructure

Your Amazon infrastructure will consist of the type of cloud you choose to deploy, the virtual networking topology you choose, security filters that you institute, the base AMIs you choose to deploy, and settings specific to any of the Amazon products that you choose to utilize. This layer needs to be approved and architected first, as ultimately the rest of your deployment will depend on a sound Amazon infrastructure.

The following figure highlights some considerations at the Amazon infrastructure layer of a SharePoint 2010 deployment:

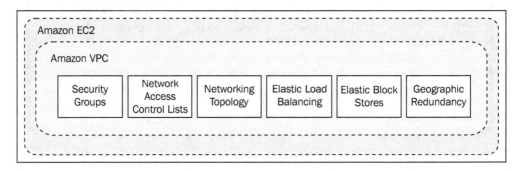

Windows infrastructure

Once your Amazon infrastructure is ready, you can move on to architecting all of the supporting Microsoft infrastructure services that SharePoint will need. This will include configuring all of the server instances created from the AMIs, integrating with Active Directory Directory Services (ADDS), building a sound DNS topology, determining and implementing the appropriate authentication and authorization mechanisms, integrating with monitoring, backup, antivirus, and other infrastructure management services.

The following figure highlights some considerations at the Windows infrastructure layer of a SharePoint 2010 deployment:

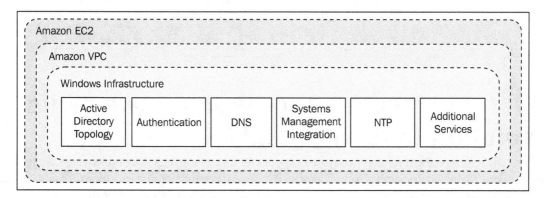

SharePoint infrastructure

You've finally reached the *application layer* of your cloud-based deployment roadmap. The Amazon infrastructure is available, your Windows infrastructure has been provisioned, and it's time to finally focus on the actual SharePoint deployment. At this point in the game you are ready to dive into capacity planning, authentication requirements, service application scaling, SharePoint security, and so on. Basically, it's time to apply everything you learned about in the previous chapter and more. Of course this is not an isolated exercise; there will be dependencies and constraints that will be dictated by or will directly impact the Amazon and Windows infrastructure layers. Be careful of the decisions you commit to. As an example, consider geographically distributed SharePoint farms. Although discussed as part of the overall SharePoint topology, this is a concept that would require architectural decisions at all three layers. If certain choices were already made and paid for at the Amazon and Windows infrastructures, then the SharePoint topology would be subject to these constraints, or the supporting layers would be subject to a re-architecture. Either way this would be a costly proposition.

The following figure highlights some considerations at the SharePoint layer of a SharePoint 2010 deployment:

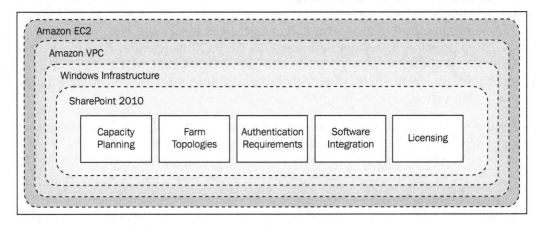

Q: Can I create a Microsoft private cloud solution for SharePoint?

A: As discussed earlier, private clouds typically use resources that are owned by and dedicated to your organization. Many vendors now offer private cloud solutions to facilitate the creation of private clouds including Eucalyptus, VMWare, and Microsoft. Let's review some of the characteristics of a Microsoft private cloud.

Technology Stack

Microsoft private cloud solutions are built using Windows Server with Hyper-V and the **System Center Suite**. The combination of these two provides enterprise-class virtualization and end-to-end service management. Specific enabling software would include:

- Windows Server
- Hyper-V
- Forefront Endpoint Protection
- System Center Suite

With the appropriate hardware and software infrastructure in place, you would be able to launch your SharePoint environment in a private cloud, exclusively created using Microsoft technologies.

Licensing

A Microsoft private cloud solution can be licensed through the **Microsoft Enrollment for Core Infrastructure** licensing program. This is a **Microsoft Enterprise Agreement (EA) enrollment**, which allows a simple and flexible per processor licensing model. It is available in three flavors: Datacenter, Enterprise, and Standard. **ECI Datacenter** is recommended solely for the fact that it supports unlimited virtualization rights.

Benefits

A Microsoft private cloud is worth considering as a full, comprehensive, end-to-end cloud computing solution. It provides a familiar and consistent platform, where your organization can potentially leverage some of the investments and skill sets that it already has.

A Microsoft private cloud solution provides cross-platform support for multi-hypervisor environments, non-MS operating systems, and a variety of application frameworks, and supports integrated automation across third-party management toolsets. It also gives your organization the flexibility to span environments and create hybrid clouds using a broad portfolio of Microsoft technologies:

- Virtualization (Hyper-V)
- Identity management (Active Directory/ADFS)
- Systems management (System Center Suite)
- Developer tools (.NET, Visual Studio)

Q: Office 365 and SharePoint Online—how many offerings and plans are actually out there?

A: SharePoint Online is a subscription-based service that provides customers with an enterprise-grade solution for creating sites to share documents and information with colleagues and customers. SharePoint Online is one of the several cloud services offered as part of Microsoft Office 365, Microsoft's premier SaaS offering.

Office 365 is also a subscription-based service that combines Exchange Online, Lync Online, SharePoint Online, and Office Professional into a cloud-based package for end users. With Office 365, users can access familiar Microsoft Office applications from anywhere, while the backend infrastructure is fully hosted, managed, and guaranteed by Microsoft.

While there are many benefits, you should ask yourself the following questions:

- Office 365 includes services other than SharePoint as part of its package. Does my organization need these additional services?

- Will Office 365 actually cost my organization less than running SharePoint on-premise?

- Office 365 does have feature and functionality limitations. Is this a deal-breaker for my organization?

 SharePoint Online, Exchange Online, Lync Online, and Office Professional Plus can also be purchased individually as standalone service plans. For additional information, refer to `http://www.microsoft.com/en-us/office365/online-services.aspx#fbid=wv13IzdlRfL`.

Office 365 has two top-level offerings: **Standard** and **Dedicated**. These two offerings are intended for different size organizations and have their own individual characteristics.

Dedicated versus Standard

Office 365 Dedicated is targeted at enterprises that do not wish to be hosted on a multi-tenant environment. This offering enables more flexibility with deployments such as farm-based solution packages and support for third-party vendor add-ons. Please note that Microsoft only offers Office 365 Dedicated to customers with more than 20,000 users.

The **Office 365 Standard** offering is intended for small and medium-size organizations. While plans are always subject to change, the current Office 365 plans are: Office 365 for small businesses and professionals (Plan P), Office 365 for midsize businesses and enterprises (Plans E1, E2, E3, and E4), Office 365 for education, and Kiosk plans (Plan K).

Small businesses

Designated as Plan P, this SharePoint offering emphasizes content sharing rather than collaboration. Plan P is intended for a small number of users, up to 50. Plan highlights include basic online document viewing, editing, and mobile access using Office Web Apps, e-mail and calendaring with Exchange Online, basic public SharePoint site and content sharing with SharePoint Online, instant messaging with Lync Online, antivirus and anti-spam filtering with Forefront Online, and so on. Please note that this plan does not include Office Professional Plus, the capability of Active Directory integration, e-mail archiving, or any live customer support.

Midsize businesses and enterprises

The **Enterprise Plans** are progressively more expensive than Plan P, but include more options; their features are generally cumulative.

- The E1 plan adds advanced administration capabilities, Active Directory integration, 24/7 support, and license rights to access on-premise deployments of Exchange, SharePoint, and Lync Server

- The E2 plan adds the ability to view, edit, and share content created in Word, Excel, PowerPoint, and OneNote desktop applications online with Office Web Apps

- The E3 plan adds Office Professional Plus, Visio Services, Access Services, rich forms for SharePoint Online, advanced archive capabilities, unlimited e-mail storage, and hosted voicemail

- The E4 plan adds enterprise voice capabilities to replace or enhance a PBX with Lync Server on-premise

Education

The **Microsoft Office 365 for Education** plan is similar to the E3 plan for midsize businesses and enterprises.

Kiosk Plans

The **Kiosk Plans** are designed for "kiosk" workers, who typically share terminals with other workers and only spend approximately 5-10 percent of their day sending e-mail or accessing company information. Typical examples of such workers include retail associates, manufacturing workers, and mail couriers. They have never had access to enterprise e-mail or collaboration platforms, so these plans are a good way to potentially improve productivity by introducing a common platform for light communication and collaboration.

- The K1 plan introduces e-mail, access to a company portal, and the ability to view Office documents

- The K2 plan adds Office Web Apps editing capabilities

Q: What authentication options do I have for SharePoint Online?

A: If deciding on an Office 365 plan, you also need to consider how your organization's end users are going to access their new SaaS offering. Identity management and authentication is a comprehensive topic whose nuances are outside the scope of this handbook, but the following general information will help you get started. For SharePoint Online, Microsoft basically offers three different types of authentication mechanisms:

- Microsoft Online Services IDs
- Microsoft Windows Live IDs
- ADFS 2.0 and Single Sign On (SSO)

> Microsoft also has a product called Forefront Identity Manager 2010, which can be integrated for managing identities, credentials, and identity-based access policies. For more information, refer to http://www.microsoft.com/en-us/server-cloud/ forefront/identity-manager-overview.aspx.

Microsoft Online Services IDs

Microsoft Online Services accounts can be created within Microsoft Office 365 and are used for end user authentication. This is the simplest option because accounts are brand new, but can lead to confusion with your end users, since they now have an additional account and password pair that they need to remember.

Microsoft Online Services IDs can be created manually through the browser-based interface, via file import or script, or by using the Active Directory synchronization tool, which will propagate your on-premise end users into Office 365. Note that this last approach will only create a copy of your end users' on-premise accounts; they will still need to remember the new password, even though the logon credential appears to be the same.

Microsoft Windows Live IDs

SharePoint Online also allows the use of **Windows Live IDs** to access the environment. This is ideal for external users and allows organizations to essentially create collaborative extranet environments. All the end user needs is their personal Windows Live ID or a Microsoft Online ID from another tenant, and your organization can grant them direct access to a site collection.

There are functional, licensing, and cost caveats, so be sure to research if this authentication mechanism is a viable option for your organization.

ADFS 2.0 and SSO

In order to create single sign-on between your on-premise domain and Office 365, you will need to employ **Active Directory Federation Services (ADFS 2.0)**. ADFS is a core Microsoft service that gives you the ability to federate your on-premise identities with Office 365, so that the same credentials are used between systems and the end users don't need to remember different passwords. Note that implementing ADFS will require additional on-premise resources, since the setup can range from single-server to multi-server, multi-site deployments depending on the size and setup of the organization. Although this is the most eloquent authentication solution, it is also technically complex and needs to be handled with due diligence and care.

Q: What about Windows Azure and SharePoint 2010? How can I take advantage of this offering?

A: Windows Azure is essentially Microsoft's operating system in the cloud. It is a PaaS offering that is starting to play an increasing role in the integration between cloud-based and on-premise solutions and services. The key difference between Azure and the other cloud options is that it does not involve actually hosting your SharePoint infrastructure in a public or private cloud. Rather, you are integrating your existing SharePoint infrastructure with additional capabilities and services offered through Azure to provide a richer experience for your end users. By integrating with Azure, you can potentially offset data costs, create efficient and reusable services, and extend your reach through wider service availability.

As an example, consider the case of Point8020 Limited, a learning content provider that utilized Windows Azure for storing and delivering video content, integrated with SharePoint 2010 to present the content in the form of embedded videos for end user training. The full case study can be found at `http://www.microsoft.com/casestudies/Case_Study_Detail.aspx?CaseStudyID=4000009235`.

Let's look at some of the basic ways Windows Azure can be integrated with and complement SharePoint 2010.

Service

Your organization can reuse existing services or can deploy custom services into the Azure cloud, and then leverage them in the context of your on-premise SharePoint environment. Specific integration points for SharePoint include the following:

- You can store data in Azure and interact with Azure data in a SharePoint list
- Your organization can model data consumed from Azure or build external lists with SQL Azure
- Web Parts can pull services or data from Azure
- Workflows and event receivers can be extended through Azure data and services
- You can integrate Azure data with SharePoint data

Data

Windows Azure provides multiple storage options, and can act as a durable repository for your organization's data. By storing data in Azure, you can benefit from persistent, redundant storage, and integration with the **Windows Azure Content Delivery Network**. Sample uses include:

- Utilizing BLOB storage for video, audio, and images
- Querying data from cloud-based or on-premise SharePoint environments
- Using Azure to store migrated or mirrored data from your on-premise environment
- Using SQL Azure for relational databases
- Federating Azure data for SharePoint search

Funny you should say that...

This section answers some typical follow up questions that you may have once you start to think about the different cloud computing options and potential deployment scenarios.

Q: Security is always a concern. What can I do to secure my SharePoint deployment in the cloud?

A: Security in the cloud computing world is still a major concern for many organizations. It is an expansive topic that can't be thoroughly covered in this tiny guide. However, we can provide some guidance to get you thinking about potential options. Let's use a SharePoint deployment in an Amazon VPC to illustrate some of these concepts. At the macro level, we can divide security concepts into two general categories:

- Amazon security
- SharePoint security

Amazon security

Amazon provides us with a few constructs that we can use to help secure our infrastructure. These include **Security Groups, network Access Control Lists (ACLs)**, and **Amazon Identity Access Management (Amazon IAM)**.

- **Security Groups**: These can be used to help secure the SharePoint servers within our Amazon VPC by specifying both inbound and outbound network traffic to and from each SharePoint server or category of server.

- **Network ACLs**: These can be used to allow or deny network traffic entering and exiting each subnet in your deployment. Host-based firewalls can also be launched as additional instances in the VPC as another layer of inspection.

- **Amazon IAM**: This enables you to securely control access to the Amazon services and resources your SharePoint environment utilizes.

SharePoint security

We can further subdivide SharePoint security into two general categories: **Data in Transit** and **Data at Rest**.

- **Data in Transit**: To secure data communication between servers in our VPC, we can implement the following options:
  - Enforce 128-bit SSL encryption for remote desktop protocol (RDP) connections
  - Enforce SSL for all client connections to the SQL servers

- ○ Enforce HTTPS (SSL) for all client connections to SharePoint services
- ○ Configure and enforce all servers to use IPSec (Internet Protocol Security) connections

- **Data at Rest**: To secure Data at Rest, we can implement the following solutions:

  - ○ **BitLocker**: Native Windows Server 2008 solution, which can be used to encrypt all SharePoint application logs, indexes, and confidential data on Amazon Elastic Block Store (Amazon EBS) volumes
  - ○ **Transparent Data Encryption (TDE)**: Native SQL Server 2008 Enterprise feature encrypts databases, log files, any information written to TempDB, snapshots, backups, and mirrored DB instances

Q: How do I migrate my on-premise deployment to SharePoint Online? What are my options?

A: Mainstream SharePoint adoption took place with Microsoft Office SharePoint Server 2007, with the majority of SharePoint deployments being on-premise deployments. At that time, cloud-based computing was not as pervasive and initial offerings were deficient in their features so hosted environments were the preferred alternative. As cloud computing has become more mature and attractive as a deployment option, many organizations are starting to consider migrating their environments. Migrating on-premise SharePoint to SharePoint Online is the most common scenario and, while all the migration scenarios will be unique due to the nature of the SharePoint platform, there are some general techniques to consider. In the order of ascending complexity, these techniques include:

- **Manual Migration through the GUI**: This is the most straightforward approach, especially for organizations that don't have a lot of content. It is free and easy, but can be time-consuming since it is done on a site-by-site and library-by-library basis. Note that all of the sites, lists, and libraries will need to be recreated and none of the original metadata or permissions will be migrated. If you have a complex SharePoint environment with content distributed across many sites, this would not be a good option for you.

- **Manual Migration via Templates**: An alternative manual method is to package the list, library, or site as a template solution and save it into your destination solution gallery. This template would contain all of the pages, libraries, lists, documents, list items, web parts, and workflows. As always, certain limitations and caveats apply including the default allowable template size, the SharePoint Online maximum file upload size, inability to save subsites, potential issues with custom web parts and workflows, stripped metadata, and so on. Be sure to thoroughly investigate all of the limitations and how they might impact your target goals.

- **Mailing and Restoring Content Databases**: This option is only available for the SharePoint Online Dedicated hosting model. Essentially this is a "dump and restore"; it requires you to back up your on-premise content databases and mail them to Microsoft who will, in turn, handle the restoration of your content into your SharePoint Online farm. If the databases are small enough, they can be sent over a secure WAN link. If the databases are large, you will need to ship them on external hard disks. Microsoft assumes a simple, out of the box SharePoint on-premise site, and will not restore your content if it doesn't meet its supported capacity guidelines. Be sure to review these guidelines thoroughly before mailing your data. Sample constraints include content databases being less than 200 GB, less than 250,000 sites per site collection, and so on. In addition, configurations that are not stored in content databases (such as audiences, profiles, and search settings) will need to be explicitly communicated to Microsoft. Custom managed paths are not supported, custom web parts are likely to fail, and all explicit customizations are subject to Microsoft approval. Planning ahead is a must.

- **Third-party migration tools**: Third-party migration tools support gradual migrations, hybrid scenarios, the reorganization of content, and the ability to migrate from different sources. However, they can be expensive and there are a limited number of viable vendors. Also, different capabilities exist depending on your version of SharePoint Online, standard or dedicated. For example, AvePoint's DocAve for SharePoint Online can migrate workflows, alerts, personal views, wiki pages, and master pages to SharePoint Online Dedicated. However, the same product cannot migrate these objects to SharePoint Online Standard. Some products such as Metalogix Migration Manager will only work with SharePoint Online Dedicated, as it requires the installation of approved agent software on the SharePoint servers. Additional vendors offering migration solutions include Quest Software, MetaVis, and Idera.

However, note that there are scenarios where not all content needs to be migrated to the public cloud. An organization might want to maintain some content on-premise and some in the cloud. Yes, we are referring to a hybrid cloud. There are many reasons why this could be. Some organizations might want to migrate their SharePoint environments gradually rather than all at once. Some SharePoint environments might be so sprawled that they could only be migrated gradually. Other organizations might want to publish content publicly in an extranet scenario, while keeping their internal infrastructures isolated. Some firms might have architectural reasons for retaining a hybrid farm: backup and failover, disaster recovery, geographic synchronization, and so on. Whatever the reason, it is a deployment model that is readily available and is worth your consideration.

Q: I've been told that SharePoint online has less features than its on-premise counterpart. What is it missing?

A: SharePoint Online does have specific limitations in terms of storage, customization, and functionality. The different plans explicitly specify limits in terms of users and storage, and customization is generally limited to SharePoint Sandboxed Solutions, approved classes and methods, and resource quotas. When creating your deployment roadmap, be sure to thoroughly review the individual offerings and the Office 365 for Enterprise Service Descriptions. That said, some of the most important features missing from SharePoint Online are:

- Business Intelligence Center, PowerPivot, PerformancePoint Services, and integration with reporting services
- Business Data Connectivity Services
- FAST Search
- Records Center
- Word Automation Services
- Secure Store Service
- Custom iFilters other than PDF not supported
- Integration with and access to LOB data is not supported
- E-mail Enabled Document Libraries
- Limited changes to public-facing websites and MySite customizability

Please note that an exact list of all missing capabilities can be found in the Service Description for SharePoint Online. Missing features can potentially be introduced into the offering over upcoming service releases.

Digging deeper

Although this chapter was technically exhausting, you might be wondering where you could find more information, at least about a specific topic covered previously. This section lists some reputable recommended sites, which will help you dive deeper into the concepts we discussed.

Amazon Web Services

- Amazon Elastic Compute Cloud: `http://aws.amazon.com/ec2/`
- Amazon Virtual Private Cloud: `http://aws.amazon.com/vpc/`
- Whitepaper–Amazon's Corporate IT Deploys SharePoint 2010 to the AWS Cloud `http://d36cz9buwru1tt.cloudfront.net/AWS_Amazon_SharePoint_Deployment.pdf`

Private Clouds

- Microsoft Private Cloud: `http://www.microsoft.com/en-us/server-cloud/private-cloud/`
- Whitepaper–Microsoft Private Cloud: `http://download.microsoft.com/download/A/D/9/AD9E9446-D20C-42DE-8FD7-2352C1D15518/Microsoft_Private_Cloud_Whitepaper.pdf`

Office 365

- Online services/SharePoint Online: `http://www.microsoft.com/en-us/office365/sharepoint-online.aspx`
- Office 365 Plans: `http://www.microsoft.com/en-us/office365/plans.aspx`
- Office 365 For Enterprise Service Descriptions: `http://www.microsoft.com/download/en/details.aspx?id=13602`
- Whitepaper–Office 365 SharePoint Online - Architectural considerations: `http://www.avepoint.com/assets/pdf/Office365_SharePoint_Online_Architectural_Considerations.pdf`

Migration

- Microsoft Online Services Transition Center: `http://www.microsoft.com/online/transition-center_before.aspx`

Windows Azure

- SharePoint and Azure Integration: `http://www.microsoft.com/windowsazure/scenarios/sharepoint-integration/`

- Learning Content Provider Uses Cloud Platform to Enhance Content Delivery: `http://www.microsoft.com/casestudies/Case_Study_Detail.aspx?CaseStudyID=4000009235`

Summary

This chapter covered the different cloud deployment models and the technologies through which they can be realized. The cloud heralds a new computing era, with potential application and cost savings to businesses of any size. Your SharePoint deployment roadmap may have just gotten more complicated, and you may be thinking "the sooner my organization embraces the inevitable, the quicker we'll realize the benefits and stay ahead of the curve". After all, the only constant in technology is change.

But you can counter this thought and ease your mind by also acknowledging that the more things change, the more they stay the same. Consider the following points:

- Business will always want to do more with less, be leaner and more agile (this seems to be the mantra of the new economy).

- Are costs really decreasing or are you really just outsourcing work to a third party?

- Does SharePoint cloud computing really add value to your business?

- Is this change improvement or change for the sake of change?

We've discussed Amazon Web Services and what they can do for SharePoint, reviewed the different plans and respective features offered through Office 365, flirted with Windows Azure, and even sampled a Microsoft private cloud solution. We've also reviewed potential security options, authentication mechanisms, and known cloud limitations. The information contained in this chapter is in no way comprehensive, but it should be enough to get you moving in the right direction. With what you now know, you should be able to identify elements in your deployment roadmap that could greatly benefit from cloud-computing. We can tell you what your technical options are, but only you know where the potential lies for your organization, and where the greatest synergy can be realized.

In the next chapter, IT trends and how they relate to the SharePoint platform are discussed. This is an important subject because SharePoint does not operate in a vacuum, isolated from the rest of the business environment. Quite the contrary, it integrates with existing deployed technology stacks, and assimilates with and evolves business process.

5

SharePoint and Important Trends

One thing that will never change is that the amount of information available will always steadily increase. In fact the amount of writing produced on a daily basis discussing IT trends, how to plan for IT trends, and how IT trends can provide benefit your organizations is a great example of this ever-changing and growing information.

The problem with IT trend information is that the writers (many of whom are not using the technology), thought leaders and analysts are barely able to keep up with the blistering pace of technology innovation, divergent needs of consumer and corporate worlds, and rapid economic change. If the authors themselves have trouble keeping up, what are the chances we, as 60-hour-a-week-working IT decision makers will be able to keep up? Also authors of trends in the media often have opinions of a technology.

This chapter allows you to understand a few key IT trends, how to plan for them, and how they can benefit your SharePoint investment.

Research by AIIM stated that half of SharePoint implementations proceed without a clear business case (which shows lack of direction from the start); only 22 percent of organizations provide users with any guidance on corporate classification and use of content types and columns; one-third of organizations have no idea as to how to use SharePoint, while one-fourth of organizations say IT is driving it with no input from information management professionals.

So there is definitely a lack of **Information Architecture (IA)** planning out there with the result of fancier and more expensive sets of shared drives rather than usable ECM systems with findable information assets.

Q: How big is SharePoint to Microsoft?

A: In the press you will often read:

SharePoint is the fastest selling product in Microsoft history.

Microsoft has been adding 20,000 SharePoint users per day, every day for the last five years.

There are over 65,000 SharePoint customers who have purchased SharePoint (statistics stated at the Microsoft SharePoint Conference in 2011: http://www.microsoft.com/Presspass/exec/kurtd/10-03-11SharePoint.mspx*).*

Further analysis may question these numbers, but there is no doubt that SharePoint is an extremely large and successful source of revenue for Microsoft, as well as being strategically important, as it helps sustain other Microsoft franchise products such as Office and Windows.

> One of the reasons the Office franchise is still relevant in a web-based world of work can be partially attributed to SharePoint's success within the enterprise. With higher reported revenue than any other division (14.124 billion dollars in 2011 according to Microsoft), the business division is extremely important to Microsoft and is primarily driven by Microsoft Office sales, which benefit from SharePoint upgrade and release cycles.

So what does this mean for your business? It means that SharePoint is not going away anytime soon, and a growing number of companies are adopting the Microsoft stack of technologies and integrating Office and SQL to continue to get greater return on their initial SharePoint investments. In fact, this integration trend is only going to increase with new product releases of SharePoint, Office, Windows, and other Microsoft products.

Q: Which IT trends matter?

Who would have thought that along with the Volkswagen Beetle and the Sony PlayStation, the Apple iPad would be one of the most successful product launches in economic history? How does this relate to the SharePoint product and other IT products in your organization?

A: There are four trends that are extremely important for every organization that you will go over in this chapter.

- **User-experience trends**: SharePoint is a tool that is often rolled out to all enterprise employees of an organization. For this reason, changes in the ways that people interact with interfaces have a significant influence on your SharePoint decisions. Many employees have high expectations for how intuitive, user friendly, and interactive the interface should be based on their experiences with popular consumer websites, devices, and technologies. Within the enterprise it can be especially challenging to keep the design up-to-date with growing user expectations.

- **IT delivery trends**: Not only is SharePoint designed for technical solutions developed by IT, but it is also designed for business solutions developed by the business. This mix creates a strong incentive for IT to understand IT delivery trends to ensure they remain relevant and continue to meet the business expectations.

- **Collaboration and communication trends**: SharePoint is often called a "collaboration platform" and often this is one of the primary focus areas for its use. It is critical that you understand key trends in the industry around collaboration such as social and unified communication.

- **Data and information trends**: With the extreme growth rate of information and the rate of change in how individuals and organizations consume and leverage that information, it is important to understand trends around information and data within the enterprise.

These trends are important because they typically relate to all deployed technologies, not just SharePoint.

There are quite a few trends that go beyond the scope of this book that can impact SharePoint strategy and future planning. In particular, if you are in a highly regulated industry, then security, compliance, and privacy trends might be far more relevant and important to you. Even the trends you do cover won't be in great depth, as it would take several chapters to explain them effectively. However, by focusing on these four, you should be confident that by the end of this chapter, you will understand a little bit more about the current challenges and market forces that will impact your existing or future SharePoint investments.

If you really want to understand related technology trends and their impact on SharePoint, be sure to carefully research and read over analyst reports (Real Story, Gartner, Forrester, IDC, and so on), industry news sites (CMSWire, AIIM, and so on), and get involved in regional technology groups (SharePoint Saturdays, AIIM chapters, SharePoint user groups, and so on) where you can share your experiences and challenges with other IT decision makers who are also struggling.

Q: What are the user experience trends?

A: User experience has always been important and good or bad user experience can make or break a system. You might implement the most technically effective solutions in the world, but if no one adopts or uses them, then they won't do anyone any good.

A common observation by the authors is that users complain that the SharePoint interface is confusing and complex, and some more mature organizations will even point out existing usability issues and challenges within the platform.

 A common example is how the Search Center and MySites do not use the same global navigation and page layouts that publishing and team sites use.

Typically users desire the interface to "not look like SharePoint" and be more like the Apple website or other popular websites.

The popular SharePoint branding website TopSharePoint (`www.topsharepoint.com/`) has hundreds of examples of public facing websites, which contain many features and design elements that many publishing-based SharePoint intranets also possess after custom branding has been applied.

 Did you know that there are over four times the number of visual designers working on the next version of SharePoint, compared to SharePoint 2010. Ask Microsoft; it is true!

Think about how users consume simple information within the organization.

Let's say it is the anniversary of your company. You want to communicate it to your employees. How would you go about this?

What's important here is that regardless of what you do to communicate, and even how you communicate, users have an expectation that they can choose how and when to consume that information. The user experience involved in consuming that anniversary information has more options and flexibility now than it had only a few years ago (if this isn't the case, then you should be concerned).

Users choose their interface and the sources for those interfaces

Users often have multiple ways in which they can receive and interact with information. To appropriately meet the increasing demands of users for more choices and personalization in how they consume information, IT needs to understand the ways SharePoint can be personalized and how users can consume information using SharePoint. By 2015, employees will customize 90 percent of the technology they use at work, according to Gartner (http://knowledge.wharton.upenn.edu/article.cfm?articleid=1937). SharePoint provides the ability to personalize the content and page design of its sites, which can be done using SharePoint's built-in alerts. Users are also able to view SharePoint information on their mobile devices or in a variety of RSS readers, such as IE or Outlook on their desktop.

SharePoint will continue to provide new ways for users to connect with and consume information within the platform. As an example, **PivotReader** (which is a way of visualizing and searching through a large collection of images – http://www.microsoft.com/silverlight/pivotviewer/) is available now and is also anticipated to be available in future versions of SharePoint. Another example is the work Microsoft Research has been doing on interesting ways of visualizing relationships and search, called **Acing,** which will create a dynamic map of people that an individual has recently e-mailed or shared MySite content with. It is important to always plan on enabling these options and making users aware that they exist.

Users choose between desktop, web, mobile, and other forms of technology-driven information consumption

This isn't a new trend. Though mobile is certainly becoming more important, for the past few versions of SharePoint there have always been options to interact with information through web interfaces and on client applications. While the browser-based web interface was the primary method for interaction through Microsoft tools such as SharePoint Workspace (formerly Groove) and Microsoft Office, users have been able to interact with and consume SharePoint data in client applications for some time.

Mobile, tablet, and other forms of consumption have had mixed experiences

While SharePoint internal environments support a mobile-friendly mode, the same feature doesn't work for anonymous users on public-facing websites. In addition to this, there is the challenge of much smaller resolutions, for which SharePoint has not been optimized. Even the web pages developed within SharePoint are large, and according to some experts, "bloated" with additional content that often is not applicable for anonymous users.

There are workarounds for all of these issues (and more), but most require some level of customization or code. So while optimizing SharePoint sites for mobile and tablet devices is possible, it isn't necessarily easy. There are quite a few documented issues (almost all of which relate to the mobile browser and the fact that SharePoint 2010 has not been designed to behave with all touch-based interfaces), which are a good reason for concern when many businesses are seeing considerable growth and adoption of tablets.

According to the JP Morgan Analyst Group, *The tablet market is expected to grow to $35 billion by 2012* (`http://www.reuters.com/article/2011/02/28/us-tablets-research-jpmorgan-idUSTRE71R3WK20110228`). Let us assure you that a big contributor to that growth will be enterprise customers who use SharePoint and will be adopting tablet devices. Microsoft is making related investments in SharePoint and Windows to tackle this more effectively (such as the Windows 8-based UI changes), but currently it is an identified challenge in SharePoint 2010.

One browser doesn't rule them all

In addition to mobile-device browser support, more and more organizations are supporting non-IE browsers. The good thing here is that SharePoint 2010 is much more cross-browser compliant than previous versions. While it no longer supports IE 6 it does support Firefox and Safari (to understand that support limitations exist, be sure to visit the Microsoft Tech Net Resource entitled "Plan browser support" at `http://technet.microsoft.com/en-us/library/cc263526.aspx`). With extra design resources (four times as many) on the next version of SharePoint, expect this support for additional browsers to increase greatly.

Growing screen resolutions and growing accessibility expectations

Beyond smaller mobile resolutions, you also have to plan for larger desktop resolutions on wide-screen monitors. This is especially relevant for many branded implementations of SharePoint. While your customized design might work fine on a standard 1024 pixels by 768 pixels resolution, it may waste a space on wider resolutions if using a static design, or may not effectively maintain the design when viewed in larger resolutions.

Accessibility has always been important, but over the past few years it has had growing support within the enterprise. Some believe it is due to the average age of employees increasing as the majority of "baby boomers" begin to have visual impairments or other challenges that correlate to age. Whatever the reason it is clear that **Web Content Accessibility Guidelines (WCAG)** are being met by more and more business solutions and are even becoming mandatory in some organizations.

Q: What are the IT delivery trends?

A: In order to keep up with external pressures on IT and the increased capabilities of competitors, IT must deliver solutions to the business more rapidly, with more value and, in many cases, without additional resources.

What is causing all of this pressure on IT? Let's take a look:

- Business cycles are shorter. There is less focus on long term planning and, due in part to the current economic turbulence, there is a strong focus on cost containment and cost reduction in most companies. Obviously in some sectors, such as the finance sector, governance and compliance are still important.

- Users have even greater levels of autonomy within the enterprise. There are fewer barriers to accessing technology solutions. These two factors often lead to unsanctioned technology purchases and uses.

- Technology is being innovated faster than ever before. Many of these technologies are disruptive and introduce new methods of interacting, and new considerations for security and manageability. With the pace of release management, it is common for release patch management to be monthly and not quarterly.

- Within the technology industry, you have entered an era of unprecedented options for SharePoint implementation, such as hosting options like on-premise, hosted or cloud.

One trend that never changes is that whatever decision IT makes, the business has to work with the decision.

One of the final interesting trends in the industry around IT delivery is the stronger emphasis on technology and solution marketing within the enterprise. This is especially true for many SharePoint implementations and projects.

In the recent OpenText/Global 360 SharePoint survey (`http://www.becauseprocessmatters.com/survey-says-lack-of-business-strategy-among-top-concerns-of-sharepoint-deployments/`), the most challenging issue cited with SharePoint was adoption and training. This challenge is related to unclear business strategy and poor alignment with real business needs. With the challenges that adoption presents, it is critical for marketing and communication to work with IT and ensure the internal messaging is clear and effective. This is especially true when many unsanctioned competitive alternatives are available for users (Box, Google, and so on). Often this can be more challenging if SharePoint was not carefully evaluated and compared against competitive technologies when selecting it in the first place.

One of the interesting results of more cloud or software-as-a-service based systems has been the increase of "business applications" or "business solutions" rather than technology-focused solutions. To provide a bit of context, consider the growing number of solutions that are now targeted at both IT and the business that, instead of focusing on the technically robust nature of the platform or product, are focusing on the specific business challenges and solutions mitigated or resolved by the solution.

Q: What are the collaboration and communication trends?

A: Every business, regardless of its size, understands the importance of collaboration and communication. Businesses are becoming more global, often dispersed across multiple locations, and the frequency and volume of virtual/remote team work is growing every year.

Even as this chapter is being written, I have **Lync Communicator** running, where I am troubleshooting a technical issue; **Outlook** is open with new e-mails from people across the world popping up every few minutes; I am working with other authors on this document on a **SharePoint** site; and even my VoIP phone is on speaker mode waiting on hold for a specific SharePoint hosting company's response to a licensing question I have. This is an example of the *always on* mentality of many people in today's world. At home or abroad, you are always connected to your work and co-workers.

Like it or love it, this is the future. The blurring between the corporate world and your personal lives is not new. You now work at home and shop at work.

 It is also rare for organizations not to have their SharePoint environments available externally (through the firewall), which further supports the growing remote workforces found in businesses today. When considering what your external unified communication strategy is, do not forget the importance of SharePoint being externally available as well.

Gartner predicted that by 2011, 10 percent of all information technology spending would reside with employees. The result of this spending could very well be that employees would pay for and bring their own technology to work.

You live in a world where collaboration and communication is the lifeblood of both your companies and your personal relationships. One of the most important things you should recognize when discussing collaboration and communication is that there is a blurring line between consumer collaboration and communication tools and those of the enterprise, so enterprise tools have to work with personal ones.

There are a number of reasons for why this might be happening at an increasing rate. Here are a few of them:

- There is a growing expectation of "always being available" and so there is less desire from employees to have multiple phone numbers, phone plans, and phones.

- Personal mobile devices such as smartphones and tablets are quickly evolving into sophisticated computers with keyboards and increasing amounts of memory. With decreased costs and almost every employee now having their own personal smartphone it makes sense that fewer employees could require the sophisticated corporate smartphones provided by many companies.

- As smartphones and tablets enter the workplace in growing numbers, IT departments are now being forced to develop personal device policies and support more than ever before.

SharePoint has been designed to be closely integrated with Microsoft's unified communication product — Lync — through the use of presence indicators and contact cards. This allows users to quickly enable voice calls or web conferences as needed from within SharePoint. It is also often useful to see the presence of certain individuals within SharePoint as you might be tempted to message a specific user about a document or piece of content within SharePoint that they modified or created.

This integration between the instant messaging, web conferencing, voice, and SharePoint is just the beginning. Connecting Lync to key workflow activities in SharePoint is one way of adding further value. In fact, Microsoft has demonstrated an instant message being sent from SharePoint to a user on Lync's instant messaging client. The user interacted with SharePoint by messaging SharePoint back and saying "yes" when prompted with whether they would like to view a new task's details. As a result the user was able to carry out an approval kicked off from the Lync instant message and SharePoint.

This advanced usage scenario outlines new integration between Lync and SharePoint and helps highlight the growing importance of tighter integration between the unstructured conversations and instant messaging you do with one another, and the structured activities being performed within enterprise platforms like SharePoint.

When planning your unified communication strategy it's important to note that many of the integration touch points mentioned so far are not available or are limited with Cisco solutions or other popular vendors.

Q: Do social computing technologies really help businesses, and is SharePoint really a social computing platform?

A: The simple answer is "yes" to both questions, though it is simpler to answer whether or not SharePoint is really a social computing platform than it is to answer how and why social computing, or **Enterprise 2.0**, technologies really help businesses.

 Not certain what social computing technology is? Social computing technology focuses on social interactions, and conversations performed by users. Examples of social computing technology are blogs, e-mail, instant messaging, social network services, wikis, social bookmarking, and activity streams.

Enterprise 2.0 or social computing technologies will become a 4.6 billion dollar industry by 2013 according to Gartner. Perhaps more important than the growth in this industry is the fact that while there are plenty of Enterprise 2.0 social software suites, most enterprise users are focused on "ease of use" and "addressing employee needs" far more than "colleagues preferring to use" a specific technology. In other words social technologies only become a factor in the enterprise when they clearly serve some business purpose.

In fact the majority of Enterprise 2.0 technology users (55 percent according to Forrester — `http://www.forrester.com/rb/Research/enterprise_20_user_profile_2011/q/id/60691/t/2`) in the business world prefer to use one social technology rather than multiple social technologies. This is a good thing for the world of SharePoint, as it contains many different social features. While it is less feature-rich around things like status updates, it does offer the majority of baseline social features.

There are a number of reasons organizations cite for introducing and leveraging social technology within the enterprise. The most popular are fairly broad value statements such as:

- It is perceived that social technology lowers the cost of sharing and organizing information (easier and more ways to access information). This is difficult to define, as few reliable numbers exist with the current level of industry maturity. Many of the statistics you find may be questionable and may not be suited to your company or industry.

- Social technology surfaces knowledge and networks (improved visibility of the individual).

- Social technology increases employee engagement (by allowing more participants).

- Less organization boundaries. Social technologies are rarely deployed for only specific departments or organization units. As a result of this (and the value of enterprise-wide deployments) there are traditionally less organization boundaries to "social" information such as people profiles.

- Since social interaction is tied directly to chronological relevance (in other words, when people engage in social activity there is always a relation to that activity being important at that point in time), it has a natural tendency to support quick, immediate, and current decision making activities.

- Social technology promotes end-user innovation.

- Most social technologies empower more people to contribute. Often it is not necessary to have "edit" rights for an item to add social tags or social discussions around it. This allows even readers to share feedback, ideas, or tag items on things they can see, interact with, but perhaps not modify.

- Almost every organization using SharePoint provides news articles that are shared on a regular basis on the Intranet or Portal. One of the simplest social features an organization can implement is a SharePoint blog. Structurally, replacing the way in which the organization distributes news to a blog site in SharePoint means that news articles are easier to publish and organize and it is easier for people within the organization to contribute, share, and comment on them.

 An article outlining the use of blog sites for news articles can be found here at https://www.nothingbutsharepoint.com/sites/eusp/Pages/Why-Leveraging-SharePoint-Blog-Features-for-Intranet-News-is-a-Great-Idea.aspx.

Q: What are the data and information trends and how is SharePoint meeting this demand?

A: You started this chapter discussing how information is always growing. In SharePoint implementations this is of course always true as well.

SharePoint 2010 can handle incredible information growth. While scale considerations were a dominant topic in the past with SharePoint, the improved 2010 platform (assuming it is technically architected effectively) scales extremely well. All of the previous scaling concerns brought up by the market have been dealt with based on additional improvements in SharePoint 2010 SP1 (though SQL limitations remain, such as a 2 GB maximum for file size).

Many organizations today are quickly learning how powerful and flexible business intelligence technologies are becoming. Making sense of all of the information you have available can be a daunting task. Implementing dynamic and interactive dashboards and reports that greatly improve the business's ability to react and make decisions is something that SharePoint can support quite well in the newest 2010 release.

In a way spreadsheet programs like Lotus 1-2-3 and eventually Excel could be considered some of the first **Business Intelligence (BI)** tools to be effectively mass marketed. Today Excel might be considered the most popular business intelligence tool in use. There are a number of reasons for why Excel might be the most popular BI tool (it is low cost, most users are familiar with it, and so on), but it is also important to understand what Excel is poor at.

- Doing large scale, or advanced reporting scenarios can be a challenge with Excel, especially when it involves collating multiple sources of data.
- Since Excel often involves unstructured input, it has a high chance of having non-validated data, which can lead to inaccurate observations and calculations (this **Garbage In Garbage Out (GIGO)** is not only limited to Excel, but is often especially prominent in Excel usage).

One of the most important trends in the industry is the importance of real-time data or chronological relevance of the data. It is extremely important for businesses to analyze, share, be accountable, and take ownership for the data they have available today when it is most relevant, and not several months from now when it is no longer chronologically relevant (unless you are comparing to see growth trends and other things like that).

Getting the right information to the right people in the right format and of course at the right time is important and often is the hardest part of implementing an effective business intelligence solution.

What is BI for the masses?

Microsoft uses the term "BI for the masses" which is a focused message that leverages Excel's widespread use as a reporting and calculating platform that most business users are familiar with. The term focuses on the fact that there is a growing desire for users to have more self-service business intelligence capabilities along with the more secure and more structured reports provided by IT.

Another way of thinking about BI for the masses is the idea of having an easier-to-implement, more flexible, and smaller implementation footprint approach for business intelligence than some of the traditional approaches used.

The trend of organizations looking for more self-service BI tools that are designed to put data analytics capabilities into the hands of end users has been increasing over the past few years. Numerous vendors besides Microsoft, including IBM, SAP, Information Builders, Tibco Software, QlikTech, and Tableau Software, offer BI self-service tools, and adoption will accelerate as more companies try to deliver BI capabilities while taking the burden off of IT so that the reports can be developed faster.

Of course, self-service isn't the only thing that matters when dealing with business intelligence. While it handles many of the ad hoc reporting requirements of a business, there is still a need for executive scorecards and dashboards, OLAP analysis, operational reporting, forecasting, data mining, and customer intelligence.

The Microsoft BI Stack

The following are BI tools that Microsoft makes available in or integrated with SharePoint that work to meet what Microsoft considers the full spectrum of business intelligence needs:

- Microsoft Excel and the PowerPivot Add-in for Excel
- Microsoft Visio
- SharePoint's Excel Services
- SharePoint's Visio Services
- SharePoint's PerformancePoint Services
- SQL Server Reporting Services
- SQL Server PowerView
- SQL Server Integration Services
- SQL Server Analysis Services

Leveraging SharePoint with Excel or Visio allows users to create workbooks and diagrams. In addition to this, leveraging Excel and Visio services also allows this information to be displayed and visualized in the web browser without having to load these applications. This adds considerable value to dashboards as they can be more interactive and allow the user to see data being updated and refreshed from other data sources defined in the Excel and Visio documents.

When dealing with larger sets of data, **PowerPivot** (a free Excel add-in) provides a way for users to still have "self-service" analytics like the ones they would do in Excel, but without the performance degradation challenges that Excel has.

Of course Excel, Visio, and even PowerPivot reports can be stored, accessed, and shared in SharePoint, but when the business needs advanced reporting and analysis capabilities, they can still rely on the powerful and comprehensive SQL BI stack.

Beyond using Excel and Visio Services to improve BI dashboards in SharePoint, you can also use SharePoint's **Key Performance Indicator (KPI)** capabilities for manual or simple automated KPI reporting and something called **PerformancePoint Services**.

In a nutshell, PerformancePoint Services allow the organization to build rich dashboards that pull information from a variety of data sources (SharePoint lists, Excel documents, OLAP cubes, relational data stores, and so on) with built-in, drill-down features (such as the decomposition tree), calculated metrics (using multiple data sources), and variance metrics (differences between target and actual). PerformancePoint dashboards can include scorecards, reports, and KPIs.

There are some great improvements in PerformancePoint Services in SharePoint Server 2010 over the standalone 2007 predecessor. Now that PerformancePoint Services understand and use SharePoint lists and libraries, it makes backup and recovery of data and reports simpler and enhances security by leveraging SharePoint's already robust permission management capabilities.

 Access Services, Excel Services, Visio Services, PerformancePoint Services, calculated KPIs, and chart web parts are all SharePoint Enterprise features and require enterprise licensing.

Search first, ask questions later

Search is certainly a trend experiencing rapid change in the market. Some of the changes in search relate to how the user experiences and interacts with search, and some relate to how the system indexes and ranks the information.

Earlier, Before Google the way users navigated and found the information they were looking for involved clicking through pages of links and navigation bars until they found the link referencing the document or the location of the information they were looking for. After Google when users are provided with a search box, it should return what they are looking for.

This actually works when the user provides clear and highly structured queries, or when the information has been tagged, indexed, and appropriately ranked. The trouble is that users have a falsified expectation that typing in a partial or poorly structured query should still return the result they are looking for, or that they shouldn't have to do the work of preparing the document for indexing by adding keywords and metadata.

Google's success in the consumer marketplace has created unrealistic (and poorly understood) expectations of search within the enterprise.

The number one thing that customers ask consultants when it comes to SharePoint search is "I want our search to work like Google. Can you do that?" One of the best responses to this comes from Virgil Carroll of High Monkey Consulting: "Give me six billion and a few years…".

The reality is that SharePoint search can be tuned and optimized so that it really does return the results people are looking for, but it requires an investment in effort and time from the organization to review search logs and failed queries, to add feedback opportunities on the search pages, and to consistently encourage users to fill out key metadata on documents like the title field.

Without careful diligence, search can quickly become more of a "random document generator" than an effective tool for finding information, simply because information has no searchable content such as metadata or key words.

The issue with enterprise search is that the information has to be both "put" into the right place, and have additional context in the form of metadata added to the information. This combination of the user planning and acting to improve "find-ability" is crucial for any search system to be successful within the enterprise.

SharePoint 2010 has taken great strides in improving the ability to assign default metadata based on where information is uploaded or created with default column values based on folders, document sets, managed metadata, the content type subscription process, and more. However, all of these enhancements have caveats and trade-offs and require careful information architecture in order for them to be effective. Managed metadata alone has a number of limitations (http://www. sharepointanalysthq.com/2011/06/managed-metadata-column-limitations/) that you should be aware of (no InfoPath, Office 2007, datasheet view, or SharePoint workspace support are just a few).

To help with findability challenges and adding additional context to information within SharePoint, there has been an influx of new products and tools that provide automatic classification of metadata terms. Within the **Enterprise Content Management (ECM)** industry there has been an increase in these tools as the data mining, indexing capabilities, and rule support of indexing engines has become more robust.

The idea behind an auto-classifier is that certain metadata can be inferred based on the frequency with which it turns up within the organization and within each document. Each automatic classifier should be tuned to your industry, then your business rules, and then finally based on what it found within the content. There are basically two modes for automatic classification; a supervised one, which still involves human effort based on the automatic discovery and recommendation of terms, as well as an unsupervised mode where it classifies documents without human intervention. Supervised automatic classification can be extremely useful for improving findability throughout your SharePoint implementation and can greatly reduce the time necessary to classify large sets of existing information.

When you go beyond SharePoint or use other search technologies, it's important to evaluate how well they work with SharePoint. Most still utilize SharePoint's indexing capabilities, ranking algorithms, and many of SharePoint's features, but some replace or remove SharePoint functionality as well.

SharePoint and FAST

Before you even read any further, answer this question: "Do you have a mature and stable SharePoint search implementation?" If your answer isn't yes then you probably aren't ready for FAST.

Why would you ever implement FAST instead of SharePoint Search?

- If you have over 100 million items, SharePoint search can't handle that load. So you would need to leverage FAST, which scales to over 500 million items. What you get with FAST is a much more scalable solution in terms of amount of data and handling system load. FAST scales very well on more hardware for load balancing and replication.

- You want deep refiners (that show the count beside each refiner or count more than the first 500 results when providing relevancy and refinement options). Natively SharePoint will only look up to the first 500 search results when it builds the refiners on the left-hand side of a search results page. This often leads to challenges when a user is looking for results beyond 500, but cannot find the appropriate refinement option and assumes it is not available in search. You also get modules for entity extraction (concepts), which can be useful, for example, names and places. FAST also has better language support. FAST can do **lemmatization**, which can expand your query to other forms of the words you are searching for.

- You also get a much more powerful query language (FQL) where you can boost different fields and values. One scenario could be to boost PowerPoint files for people in the marketing department.

There are other visual benefits such as document previewing and thumbnails, visual and contextual best bets, and the ability to sort and find similar results, but most of these don't encourage a business to spend the much larger license costs on FAST. Typically it is the reasons mentioned previously that have a bigger impact, especially the language and scale considerations.

Funny you should say that...

While the trends already mentioned so far in this chapter are the most prominent ones that impact SharePoint, there are a few others that are well worth mentioning. The next few trends are often discussed with very different perspectives based on experience, and while there are no clear answers, there are certainly a few important points you can make to help reduce the uncertainty you might be facing.

Q: What are the security trends?

A: One thing that SharePoint does a great job of is shining a light on all of the issues in your organization. While this can be considered a good thing, it can be very damaging if the organization isn't prepared to respond effectively.

A very common example of this is when an organization decides to index a file share and then finds a large number of documents that should be private or secured, but are actually not secured. SharePoint didn't change security, but it highlighted the existing security issue.

SharePoint permission sprawl

SharePoint permission sprawl (the uncoordinated and untrained application of permissions) is often one of the biggest challenges facing large implementations. While SharePoint security and permissions are robust and have most of the native capabilities organizations require, managing security and permissions over time (and across multiple sites or site collections) is extremely difficult with out of the box capabilities. This is also why there are product companies that specialize in providing additional security administration options for SharePoint.

It is critical for successful implementations to have clear permission guidance and to follow Microsoft recommended practices around fine-grained permissions (item-level permissions) as SharePoint performance and usability can be impacted by the permission sprawl.

For many organizations, SharePoint represents an opportunity for end users to manage their own permissions, but many organizations struggle with governing, training, and supporting this level of distributed permission management. When planning permissions, the organization should start with its existing active directory groups (when applicable) and focus on maintaining visibility and understanding for how content is being secured so that guidance, support, and policies can be updated accordingly.

Environment security

Beyond just securing the information from an individual worker level you also have to keep in mind the importance of securing the entire environment. The positive thing here is that SharePoint is based on Windows server security as well as existing firewall security. So as long as you are diligent and maintain the security at both the external and internal server layers, often the providers themselves (such as Microsoft) will provide necessary patches, updates, and upgrades to ensure the environment remains secure.

Also, SharePoint has many security hardening measures that can be put into place from the farm and sever level, all the way down to the site collection level. Of course the more secure you make things, the harder it is to keep performance and user experience high. There is a saying that a system with no users/access is the most secure system, but that also means that the system isn't providing any benefit. So find the right balance based on your own business needs.

Q: How agile is SharePoint?

A: According to Gartner, by 2012 agile development methods will be utilized in 80 percent of all software development projects. The number of organizations adopting and leveraging agile software development to improve IT is continuing to grow. IT departments are finding that by introducing agile development methods, they are able to respond more rapidly and deliver more value to the business.

What is agile?

Agile software development is a software development methodology based on iterative and incremental development, where requirements and solutions evolve through collaboration between self-organizing, cross-functional teams. It promotes adaptive planning, evolutionary development and delivery, a time-boxed iterative approach, and encourages rapid and flexible response to change.

Agile development methods work extremely well with SharePoint solutions. Why? Put simply, because SharePoint is a large and complex platform. It requires careful learning and does not follow a simple pattern where one can know everything and account for everything in planned stages. Agile development focuses on building solutions where the requirements evolve and take shape over multiple iterations, making it a much more effective set of methodologies than ones that require significant or complete understanding at the outset of the development project.

Even **Microsoft Certified Master (MCM)** and **Microsoft Certified Architect (MCA)**, the highest level of certification possible with SharePoint, admit that no one person can know absolutely everything about SharePoint. In fact the MCM motto is "know what you know, know what you don't, and never confuse the two", which is very relevant for SharePoint work.

Another of the big issues is that SharePoint involves heavy user interaction. Often the challenges faced with SharePoint solutions and implementations are not technical challenges, but instead social or business challenges. This often results in expectation management and delivery problems, which are mitigated through the user or proof of concepts iteration, and earlier user involvement (all the things Agile development methodologies do well). In other words a more linear method will be less effective than one that is iterative.

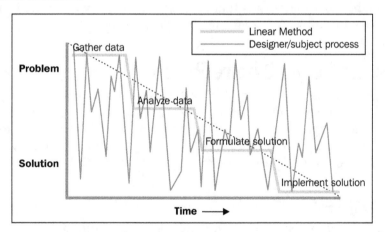

The erratic line in the previous screenshot (from Jeff Conklin's outline of wicked problems `http://cognexus.org/wpf/wickedproblems.pdf`) outlines the cognitive activity of a designer when dealing with a design or planning problem. What it symbolizes is that the (solution) designer actually learns and improves his or her understanding, even when well into the implementation phase, if dealing with wicked problems. In SharePoint, many problems are actually wicked problems and follow this same pattern of opportunistic learning.

If you recognize that developing and delivering solutions with SharePoint effectively involves many rapid iterations, proof of concepts, and prototyping where you can get more user feedback, improve your understanding, and show more demonstrable value, then agile development methodologies align well with the less defined or structured SharePoint projects and solutions.

In fact for many of your clients SharePoint development is easier when building solutions using out of the box (**OOTB**) capabilities. This usage of OOTB capability leads to reduced testing, and more rapid development cycles as well as an increase in the volume of development projects. This increase then results in the organization looking at new ways to meet the increased demand and to effectively support the growing user expectations. While no single methodology alone is the answer, there is value in using agile methodologies with SharePoint.

Q: SharePoint applications: Is it better to buy or build?

A: "It depends" is always the correct answer to this question. The advantage of buying over building relates to scale of development and cost. It is mostly much more cost effective to buy, but it reduces the control you have on the application or solution.

With SharePoint's long upgrade path of over three years between versions, the build or buy is simplified as typically a product or application will deliver value for at least the lifecycle of the current version of the product within your enterprise.

There are over 4,000 SharePoint partners in the Microsoft ecosystem. Almost every one of those partners has solutions, tools, or products that help businesses get additional value out of their SharePoint investments.

So if you are considering building instead of buying, take two steps back and re-read that statement. It is rare for someone not to have experienced your challenge, and rare in the SharePoint marketplace for a solution not to be developed and available for purchase that has been vetted or implemented with multiple clients.

The trend in the marketplace is that far more people are buying instead of building with SharePoint 2010 over previous versions. With over 1000 SharePoint solutions and products in the marketplace and over 1000 in development, this shouldn't come as a surprise. That means that there are as many solutions, products, and add-ons in development right now as there have been built in the 10 plus years SharePoint has been in the marketplace.

Beyond the economic advantage of the tool costing less to buy than build for the organization as a whole, many organizations also prefer to have the software assurance and support agreements that come with such tools. Since SharePoint has an upgrade path, it is often useful to understand the company's approach for SharePoint upgrades for each product. Since most provide upgraded versions of their products for each SharePoint version, this can also save you the internal costs necessary with having to rebuild your own customizations before each upgrade.

While there is still a strong market for SharePoint tools that simplify administration, development, and training, there is also a quickly growing market of SharePoint applications. These SharePoint applications are different from the tools or heavier products, which focus on technical challenges and limitations; the applications often focus on end-user interaction and business challenges instead. These solutions are often built and sold by services firms or companies that aren't purely product companies. As a result it is important to carefully evaluate whether these are truly turnkey solutions, or whether they are services packaged to look like a turnkey solution.

Q: What are the reasons for the rapid growth of more SharePoint applications that you can download and activate?

A: While there is speculation around SharePoint marketplaces, there are a few reasons for why this growing interest may be taking place in the industry:

- SharePoint 2010 is a more developer-friendly platform and it is much easier for developers to get started than with previous versions due to increased documentation, market maturity, better certifications, simpler tools, and more training material.

- SharePoint 2010 standardized on a consistent delivery mechanism for almost all customizations.

- Code enhancements and sandbox management enable more business units or multi-tenant/shared hosting clients to use custom applications and solutions.

- The number of organizations now using SharePoint has grown drastically over the past few years. This makes it more attractive for businesses to develop and market solutions and applications.

- According to multiple surveys from Global 360 and AIIM, more and more businesses are beginning to use SharePoint for more than basic portal or intranet scenarios. This increasing maturity is creating a greater demand for specific vertical or horizontal business solutions.

In fact the SharePoint services industry is worth well over $6 billion. Does that sound intimidating? Microsoft stated that for every $1 of licensing sold it has led to between $6-9 of services. This makes sense when you consider that strategy, infrastructure, upgrades, migrations, integration, search, and development (such as branding) are all examples of services for which organizations often leverage external expertise.

For customers, this means that there are over 4,000 (registered) system integration partners who specialize in SharePoint around the world to choose from.

This is a good thing. It means that there are more competitive prices, more local partners you can connect with, and an abundance of solutions being built on SharePoint.

If you are having a business problem, it is almost certain that another business has had that same problem. With the size and breadth of the SharePoint partner ecosystem it is also almost certain that a partner has built, or helped build a SharePoint solution for that specific business problem. The more mature and frequent the business problem, the higher the probability that there is a structured and supported product built on SharePoint that solves it.

The downside to this is perhaps more important to highlight. It is a challenge navigating the world of SharePoint consultants and solutions. SharePoint's success has led to an abundance of partners rapidly developing SharePoint practices and many organizations being sold inexperienced or ineffective SharePoint services and solutions.

If you take this abundance of applications into account with the discussions around agile development and the growth of cloud technology, it begins to paint a very rapid, iterative, and business-focused picture of how IT must deliver technology solutions to the business. This change to how IT delivers may only be focused on communication and alignment initially, but over time will lead to behavioral changes, cost-allocation changes, and entirely new ways in which IT supports the business.

Digging deeper

Information without context is sometimes not enough. It is important to do your own research and analysis so that you can come to your own conclusions the impact SharePoint has on the industry and the impact the industry has on SharePoint.

Q: What are your internal corporate trends?

A: As per experience, employees always complain about two things: cafeteria food and IT.

Cafeteria complaints	IT complaints
It doesn't have what I want.	IT can't give me what I want.
It is too expensive or it is not free.	What do you mean I have to help?
The line is always too long.	IT takes too long.
There isn't enough selection.	Don't tell me what I need.
There is too much selection.	Just tell me what I need.
The food is better next door.	I prefer this technology over ours.

While it is always useful to know what employees complain about, it is also important to understand more about what their pain points really are.

Ask your users what technology they are using. Find out if your users are working from home. Find out what they think the biggest challenges are, what they are frustrated with, and what changes they want to see. What trends are they seeing?

This information will always be far more actionable and useful than any external trend information.

Q: What are the consumer trends?

A: Keep a close eye on significant changes in the consumer marketplace. These almost always impact the business, though often in indirect ways. The most significant ones right now are social, mobile, tablet, and software as a service. In a few months there could be new concerns and trends that you as businesses need to carefully evaluate and watch when planning for the future.

To keep on top of many of these trends here are some recommended sites:

- TechCrunch: `http://www.techcrunch.com/`
- Engadget: `http://www.engadget.com/`
- Gizmodo: `http://www.gizmodo.com`
- CNN Technology: `http://edition.cnn.com/TECH/index.html`
- Forbes Technology: `http://www.forbes.com/technology/`
- Mashable: `http://www.mashable.com/`
- Wired: `http://www.wired.com/`

Did you know you can also monitor industry news through Google Alerts (`http://www.google.com/alerts`), which provides personalized e-mails based on new search results. This can simplify the delivery of new industry information as it relates to a specific topic like SharePoint. While it won't be as structured as the RSS feeds provided by the sites listed here, it can provide additional exposure to events and insights.

Q: What are other industry and technology trends?

A: Being ignorant of external forces and market impacts puts your organization at risk of not remaining competitive and ready to handle the incredible pace of change you experience in the world of technology. So be sure to read up on what is going on in the industry regularly.

Here are a few free resources to help get you started:

- CIO.com: `http://www.cio.com/`
- Harvard Business Review: `http://www.hbr.org/`
- ReadWriteWeb: `http://www.readwriteweb.com/`
- CMSWire: `http://www.CMSWire.com`
- ZDNet XE "ZDNet:URL" : `http://www.zdnet.com/`
- Focus: `http://www.focus.com/`
- Alltop: `http://cio.alltop.com/`
- GigaOm: `http://www.gigaom.com/`

If you are looking for something more comprehensive and are willing to pay for it, the following recommend:

- Gartner: `http://www.gartner.com/`
- Forrester: `http://www.forrester.com/`
- Real Story Group: `http://www.realstorygroup.com/`
- IDC: `http://www.idc.com/`
- Intranet Benchmarking Forum: `http://www.ibforum.com/`
- Jakob Nielsen: `http://www.useit.com/`

Be careful when evaluating external research reports and industry news. Keep in mind that public statistics can help, but without the entire context behind the statistic your interpretation may be inaccurate, or worse yet the statistic may be written to infer a specific interpretation that benefits someone else.

For example, in a 1000 employee company, lost productivity costs approximately $5 million a year. However you have no context as to when this statistic was determined or what its source was. In this example the statistic comes from "Hidden Costs of Information Work" written by the IDC in 2006. To fully understand the statistic and how it came about you would need to read that entire report. This statistic is outdated and shouldn't be the sort of thing you make a decision based on today.

 Generally internal statistics are far more effective and reliable than external statistics when it comes to making SharePoint investment decisions. Here are some sample internal statistics that might influence your decisions around SharePoint:

- 20 percent of your IT support people who travel do not have access to your IT policies and support documents when travelling. Source: "Support Review Q4," IT, 2011.

- Four out of five of your workers do not know that there is an employee disaster relief fund. Source: "HR Employee Benefits Survey," HR, 2011.

- Currently you pay for full licensing on seven different enterprise document management solutions. Source: "Financial Audit of Licensing Costs," Finance, 2011.

Summary

This chapter has addressed important questions and answers and analyzed key SharePoint trends to arm you with more information about why and how SharePoint can be a good investment. You went beyond simple industry adoption statistics and took a deep dive into how, when implemented and approached correctly, SharePoint delivers compounded return or value with each new version.

Remember to keep a sharp eye out for some of the current challenges SharePoint 2010 has when it comes to mobile, tablet devices, and usability so that you can control and set the right expectations with your business. SharePoint's breadth is also one of its weaknesses as it's a "Jack of all trades".

In the next few chapters, you will dig into how to develop internal resources and grow SharePoint talent and capacity within the organization. As you read these chapters, remember that industry trends go beyond SharePoint features and usage. Considerations like growth in jobs (`indeed.com` shows a 900 percent growth rate in SharePoint jobs over the last five years) and an evolving body of knowledge (there are over 400 SharePoint 2010 books on Amazon as of March 2012) require careful consideration and planning when making decisions on how and where to invest in your SharePoint implementation.

6
How to get the .NET Developers on Board Quickly?

If you look at the Microsoft Development Network (MSDN) website, `www.msdn.com`, you would think that SharePoint is just a simple extension of a .NET platform and that if your organization has .NET developers, you are set to install SharePoint and undertake even more complex software projects. However, development teams quickly realized that SharePoint requires a fair amount of specialized knowledge and different technical approaches that are unique to the SharePoint developer skill and mindset. These are discussed in *Chapter 8, Managing your First SharePoint Project*.

This chapter will discuss development issues that will help you better understand the issues of SharePoint development. We will explore the differences between .NET development and SharePoint development, the challenges and roadblocks that the developers face, and how to learn SharePoint development quickly. We will also discuss unique developer tools for SharePoint and how an organization should approach SharePoint development.

This chapter assumes that a developer is a .NET developer.

Q: What's so different about SharePoint development compared to .NET development?

A: As discussed in the previous chapters, SharePoint is a .NET Framework with extensive built-in functionality. You will often hear Microsoft describe SharePoint as a platform that you can build on. In layman's terms, SharePoint functionality could be described as a Lego set, where you can build anything you want out of the box and if certain bricks do not match your functionality, then you need to build your own brick, also known as custom .NET development. When this custom development is necessary, it must fit into the existing bricks of the solution to really leverage the functionality of these other bricks.

Because of the existing .NET Framework (the SharePoint server that your organization has purchased and installed), a true SharePoint developer will leverage SharePoint's existing functionality and extensibility model such as lists, pages, web parts, and workflows.

The SharePoint Object Model is best described at `http://sharepointobjectmodel.com/`. Although SharePoint can restrict the developer, it can also enable him/her, by providing a server platform that can be built upon.

This has significant impact on the average developer because not only are they asked to develop but also manage, configure, and maintain a server environment. Developers are thrust into infrastructure technologies such as **Active Directory**, **Internet Information Services (IIS)**, **Domain Name System (DNS)**, and other technologies that challenge the common skill sets of the average developer. In large companies this can cause problems because developers do not usually have administration privileges, yet their SharePoint deployments integrate with these infrastructure technologies.

Another major difference between SharePoint development and ASP.NET development stems from the fact that a SharePoint developer is developing for an existing framework, which has a deployment process such as **Web Solution Packages (WSP)** that allows developers to package customizations to be uploaded to and deployed by SharePoint. This SharePoint release process is different to the traditional .NET development.

SharePoint also introduces some unique tools that are dedicated to SharePoint development, such as SharePoint Designer, InfoPath, and the Office suite. All the three products provide additional functionality and are often overlooked when a developer is asked for a SharePoint approach for a business problem. SharePoint Designer is the main tool used to develop branding-related solutions, among others, and this tool allows developers to connect to existing SharePoint sites and develop and deploy custom page layouts, master pages, web parts, parts, workflows, and content that can be reused by end users. Development performed with SharePoint Designer has been referred to as a "no-code solution".

The following table identifies the main development tools provided by Microsoft for the SharePoint technology. The **Development type** column indicates the developer type:

- **Frontend .NET development**: Activity mostly using the SharePoint API framework and existing SharePoint functionality such as list and the security model. This is very configurable.

- **Backend .NET development**: Using SQL, AD, and IIS functionality. This type of development is typically for large projects that require integration to other applications.

Tool	Description	Development type
Visual Studio 2010	The main development tool used to build code solutions. Visual Studio includes SharePoint web parts, workflows, features, and other templates that developers can use to start custom development.	Backend .NET development
SharePoint Designer 2010 (Free)	Used for building no-code solutions such as master pages, layouts, workflows, web parts, and provides administrative and configuration ability.	Frontend .NET development
InfoPath 2010	Forms designer and generator. InfoPath forms can be implemented as both no-code and code solutions. Use coded InfoPath forms for complex forms that require unique functionality. Part of Office 2010.	Frontend .NET development

Tool	Description	Development type
Visio 2010	Visio can be used to diagram the basic overall functionality of SharePoint workflows. Workflow Visio diagrams can then be imported in SharePoint Designer 2010 for deployment and further development. Visio can also be used to implement Business Intelligence Solutions as Visio diagrams can consume data and then be displayed on SharePoint. Visio Services are only available for SharePoint Enterprise.	Frontend .NET development
Performance Point 2010	A built-in designer to develop scorecard, Business Intelligence, and Key Performance indicators. The designer is used to build no-code solutions and aggregate data at the click of the mouse.	Backend .NET development

There is a term *SharePoint frontend developer* that often pops up in the SharePoint world and the skill set may meet your requirements, particularly for a first project. In *Chapter 1, Defining a SharePoint IT Strategy* the SharePoint strategy roadmap example outlined that .NET development did not occur until a later phase, because frontend developer skills were required for initial requirements.

This frontend development can also include JavaScript, XML, HTML, and CSS knowledge. It is debatable if this is development, but it is customization and a skill a developer can learn and may have.

SharePoint Designer and InfoPath do not require .NET knowledge and Performance Point 2010 is only available with SharePoint Enterprise.

It is a waste of skill for a senior developer to be assigned a project that is really frontend development. Yes they maybe technical, but it's a new skill they will need to learn.

Hiring managers will often wish to hire a SharePoint developer with multiple front and backend SharePoint skills sets and end up with a generalist, rather then a specialist. This is a common mistake with hiring managers, when the role is for multiple people, rather than one person.

Other no-code solutions that are introduced by SharePoint are InfoPath development, Visio development, SQL Server Reporting Services (SSRS), and Performance Point development, to name a few. All are peripheral to .NET development but unique to SharePoint development.

Developers will be more than capable in SharePoint development if they understand these differences and know their pitfalls. The following table highlights the overlap in the skill set.

Skills	SharePoint	.NET
InfoPath	Yes	
Sites and Lists	Yes	
Deployment	Yes	
SharePoint Designer	Yes	
CAML Query	Yes	
C# or VB Languages	Yes	Yes
Core .NET Assembles	Yes	Yes
Web Services and WCF	Yes	Yes
JavaScript, HTML, Master pages, CSS, Page Layouts	Yes	Yes
Active Directory	Yes	Yes
Windows Presentation Foundation		Yes
Windows Services		Yes
Windows Form		Yes
.NET MVC		Yes
J# Language		Yes
LINQ	Yes	Yes
Windows Foundation	Yes	Yes
Page Lifecycle	Yes	Yes
Visual Studio and SQL	Yes	Yes

Notice from the table the broad SharePoint skills are frontend developer (InfoPath), infrastructure (Active Directory), and web skills (JavaScript, Master pages)

To add a final part of complexity to this answer, the developer must know the organization's SharePoint governance that they are allowed to work in. This is discussed in *Chapter 2, Just Enough Governance*. Just because SharePoint has a functionality does not mean it has been switched on to in the organization. This could include My Sites, user external access, and full Active Directory profile imports.

Q: How should we approach SharePoint development?

A: Not to answer a question with a question, but before you answer this question, you have understood that the SharePoint Designer, InfoPath, and frontend coding such as JavaScript and HTML do not meet your business requirements.

As the previous paragraphs stated, SharePoint development can be a sizable investment for organizations and it is important that your approach around development truly leverages SharePoint to provide value to the organization. So understanding the development costs of hiring expertise or providing a dedicated team for development, the cost of software licenses for development tools such as Visual Studio, Windows Server, and SQL Server are important, because return on investment questions should be asked. There are also additional hardware costs to support this development. To help support development, organizations also implement strict policies around what and how SharePoint development is implemented, such as releases and governance. Policies are in place to maintain the stability of SharePoint, minimize disruptions to day-to-day business, and define processes to ensure quality. Figuring out costs and hiring expertise might be the easier part.

The development lifecycle of a SharePoint development project is no different than that of a .NET project. Although not all organizations require development, test, and production server environments for development, it is important to incorporate several key environments to facilitate SharePoint development, testing, and delivery.

Have a source-control strategy

Although code management is not unique to SharePoint development it is essential for all custom development. Many development projects fail because of the inability to manage code that is produced by team development. There are free source-control products such as Visual Source Safe (VSS) (being phased out by Microsoft), Team City, and Concurrent Version System (CVS) to name a few. The Microsoft supported product is Team Foundation Server (TFS).

Subversion (SVN) is another development tool, but it is better for smaller teams and less complex scenarios. Git is better for large distributed teams that require offline access.

There are several advantages of using Team Foundation Server (TFS) and the authors highly recommend it as opposed to others. Firstly, TFS is integrated with Visual Studio. This means that developers can easily manage code from the developer tools they use. Other free/open source options have add-ons that will integrate to some degree to Visual Studio, but these can be limited. Secondly, TFS is SharePoint aware. This means that TFS will recognize SharePoint customizations and properly handle the unique scenarios and files only found in SharePoint development. Thirdly, TFS can be used to manage deployment. One central tool can be used to deploy to all environments. Development, testing, and deployment can be more centrally managed.

Create a development environment

A development environment is pivotal to the success of SharePoint development. This environment should include the necessary tools to support development and testing.

The environment also needs to be configured to grant developers full access to the server, to ensure that developers have the ability to make modifications to core SharePoint server files and configuration that might be required during development.

All customizations should start in development, be deployed and tested in UAT, and finally be installed and used in production. Any shortcuts and workarounds to this process are the road to late night troubleshooting with the developer team.

These rights should also include the ability to restart the server, or start and stop core services to test customizations without interfering with production environments. This is why a dedicated development environment is necessary.

Development environments should also mirror production environments in server configuration, Operating System Architecture, and SharePoint server versions. This might sound obvious, but several applications such as Visio, will only work with x64 architecture. A virtual development environment can prove quite beneficial in this scenario. If the stability of servers were compromised for any reason, a snapshot would allow you to revert back to a previous stable state of the environment. This environment should be configured for server performance and rigorous development and testing. In a perfect world this environment should be generous in memory and optimized for the developer experience. This development environment should also mirror UAT.

With Microsoft SharePoint Server 2010 there is the ability to deploy reusable packages that can contain features that are relevant to the environment. The deployment of solutions is flexible as they can be enabled or disabled individually and deployed directly onto your SharePoint Server farm, or into a sandbox. A sandbox is a restricted execution environment that enables programs to access only certain resources, and that keeps problems that occur in the sandbox from affecting the rest of the server environment. Solutions that you deploy into a sandbox, which are known as sandboxed solutions, cannot use certain computer and network resources, and cannot access content outside the site collection they are deployed in.

For more information about solutions, see Solutions Overview
http://go.microsoft.com/fwlink/p/?LinkID=156638.

Because sandboxed solutions cannot affect the whole server farm, they do not have to be deployed by a farm administrator. Sandboxed solutions can be deployed by a site collection administrator or, in certain situations, by a user who has the Full Control permission level at the root of the site collection.

Build a User Acceptance Testing (UAT) environment

A User Acceptance Testing (UAT) environment will allow developers to continue testing and to get feedback from end users. Some customizations that are developed through SharePoint Designer are performed right on the SharePoint Site. The UAT environment is a perfect environment to build these customizations and get end user feedback. This environment should not include all the development tools necessary for custom development. The main purpose is providing a production like environment. This naturally excludes the development tools that are installed in the development environment and should also include production-like content to simulate the production SharePoint Environment.

Many organizations have a plan in place to move production material to UAT and even development environments to synchronize environments. User Acceptance users have access to the SharePoint sites that are available through the UAT environment but do not normally have access to log on or access the server in any other capacity, because the technical environment is mirroring the production.

 What is sometimes different with SharePoint solutions is that the user base tests the application on UAT, so they need access to this environment. Typically with traditional .NET solutions the UAT tests are such that the code doesn't blow up.

Build a production environment

Did you notice how this is the last environment mentioned? Most organizations jump to the production SharePoint environment and neglect the previously discussed environments. Although the configurations on this environment can be self-explanatory there are a few key exceptions. There should be no custom development performed on the production environment and developers should not have access to deploy and access this server. Take the time to set up a deployment strategy around who deploys and when. Deployment to production should be very controlled as new or upgraded customizations disrupt the user experience. All deployment should be performed during the off hours (outside of the working hours) to minimize downtime. This environment should also implement a disaster recovery strategy. Disaster recovery means minimizing downtime in case servers fail or malfunction, corruptions to content occur, or any of the many other unforeseen issues occur. To describe this we would need another book.

Deployment strategy

Take the time to build a strategy around development, testing, and deployment.

Microsoft has released virtual machines that are available for download and demonstration purposes. When starting out, it is a good approach to download the available Virtual Machines, to obtain exposure to a server environment quickly.

 These virtual machines are configured for demonstration rather than development purposes.

There have been known issues for some versions of these virtual machines and these can require re-activation of the software licenses. For this reason, we do not use them and recommend building out your own personal environment to obtain an understanding of installation and the product so you can be a more effective developer. The demo virtual machines that Microsoft releases also have every known service and feature turned on; this can make those VMs quite sluggish in performance. As a developer it is simply not necessary to have every service and feature turned on and it can lead to a negative development experience when the environment is sluggish. If the demo environment is used, I highly recommend turning off features such as **Fast Search** or **Enterprise search** that are simply not used in the development experience, for the most part.

Q: What roadblocks do new SharePoint developers face?

A: SharePoint is a mammoth product with many features and many avenues of development and it can be quite intimidating when attempting to understand the entire framework. The learning curve can be substantial because SharePoint is dependent on server environments. Developers are not always used to working with and managing servers to the extent a SharePoint developer is required to do. The following table outlines key SharePoint skills that developers should have:

Essential SharePoint developer skills	Hands-on awareness	Awareness
CAML	SQL Management studio	Firewalls
.NET development (C# or VB.NET)	Visual Studio 2010	Exchange
Master Page, HTML, CSS, and JavaScript	Virtual Machine (Hyper-V or VMware)	SQL Database Mirroring
Web Services, WCF Services		
Deployment with Web Solution Packages (WSP) and SharePoint Features		

In the previous table, the skill **Awareness** such as for firewalls and Exchange, is more about being aware of the functionality and implications, rather than having access to this technology to make changes.

Before development can start, a developer needs to understand the SharePoint framework. Framework is a fancy way of saying *SharePoint out of the box functionality*.

If a developer is asked to build a custom workflow, he/she will first have to understand the bigger picture of requirements, such as:

- What a workflow looks like inside of SharePoint
- How users interact with the workflow
- Workflow steps
- Other concepts such as sites, lists, document libraries, list items, and content types

This knowledge is vital, so they can leverage the SharePoint framework and not build new .NET functionality to duplicate already existing SharePoint functionality.

> The moment the solution requires .NET development, it is a development project and there are additional complexities involved, such as source code maintenance, small requests, and environment stage releases. If this workflow can be built with SharePoint Designer then the go live date may be sooner. What you do not want to do is start the workflow deployment with SharePoint Designer and realize that the available functionality cannot meet the requested functionality and have to start from scratch.

A developer needs to understand the pros and cons of each development path in order to make sound decisions about the customization. Once the developer makes a decision about the development path he/she might need to learn how to use development tools such as InfoPath 2010 and SharePoint Designer 2010.

> A common mistake that developers often make is that they only look at the end point of the solution, rather than the SharePoint components and the path to reach this endpoint that are required for the solution, such as infrastructure, user base, or integration. So a holistic approach is essential. This development planning approach is not unique to SharePoint and this is key to a successful deployment.

Complementary SharePoint technology

Infrastructure technologies such as **Active Directory** and **IIS** go hand-in-hand with SharePoint development and can also prove to be quite a challenge. The average newbie developer doesn't work at the infrastructure level of development so they are unequipped to deal with issues that arise.

A SharePoint developer needs to understand the configuration of servers in order to develop for SharePoint, be in tune with how customizations will behave inside a multi-server farm, and know where to look if they exhibit unexpected behavior. Part of the SharePoint infrastructure is SQL, and the beginning developer will need to understand some basic SQL management, configuration, and security.

 SharePoint developers spend a considerable amount of time in infrastructure and this can be a roadblock if they are not prepared for it.

SharePoint developers need to be "big picture" focused and beginners can be unprepared to work at that level. The typical ASP.NET development team consists of a mix of junior, intermediate, and senior developers, all of whom have different responsibilities. Although the roles might be similar in SharePoint development, the responsibilities are definitely not.

 A team approach is essential. A backend developer, a frontend InfoPath developer, and a SharePoint infrastructure guy is a good combination. Levels of experience can also be applied.

A junior developer is rarely asked to deal with architecture, infrastructure, or deployment. These are mainly an intermediate or a senior developer's responsibility. In SharePoint development, we all need to understand it all at once and right from the start. Some developers, specifically beginners, struggle not only with development but also with testing, deployment, configuration, end user testing, and quality assurance, and overall functionality. SharePoint developers need to "wear different hats" depending on the situation. They are part developers, business analysts, architects, and infrastructure specialists. Although developers may also need to take on different roles, it is not as common, especially as a beginner, and dealing with all of these facets at once is also a unique challenge.

The role of wearing a good business analyst hat is essential; most often it is also likely the hardest role for a beginning developer.

The geeks need to have interpersonal skills (God help us here), but it is rare to find a developer with both technical and business analyst expertise. Yet this combination of skills is crucial for a SharePoint developer because all custom development directly affects end users. It is very rare that a SharePoint developer can focus on a development task that is disconnected from end users. A development team can help alleviate this challenge by distributing responsibilities, but there is no escaping from the fact that all SharePoint developers need to wear multiple hats and have a team approach. This challenge is discussed further in *Chapter 7, Growing SharePoint Capacity and Meeting Staffing Resource Needs*.

A developer always develops, while a SharePoint architect must build using the existing SharePoint framework, understand the business needs, and build a solution.

Beginning SharePoint developers face several roadblocks but they can be overcome. If the developer has the hunger and drive to learn new skills, he/she can make his/her way over the steep learning curve. Although no one person can completely master all of the skills SharePoint requires, motivation, ambition, and humility will help the beginning developer overcome his/her initial discomfort in order to navigate the inevitable roadblocks ahead.

Q: How do we avoid mistakes in the early stages?

A: In the attempt to provide value by delivering customizations, a developer may take shortcuts on setup that have significant impact later on. There is a reasonable amount of setup required for SharePoint development and developers should appreciate the importance of taking the time to configure the development environment.

Typically, a beginning SharePoint developer will deploy a customization to a target test or production environment and after the customization fails will say, "But it worked in my environment." That developer has failed to identify that the two environments are not the same.

Before any development takes place, the infrastructure group must take the time to set up an environment that is similar to the target environment. For example, if the target environment is SharePoint Standard, then the development environment should try to replicate that same environment. If the organization is using SharePoint Foundation 2010 it is no use developing in an environment using SharePoint Server 2010 Enterprise. A development environment will never be exactly the same, but a developer should try to mirror the target environment as closely as possible.

SharePoint is always releasing new service packs or cumulative updates but installing updates might not always be beneficial. SharePoint developers must remember that they are not creating a personal development environment but one that is dedicated to a particular target environment. The developer should make sure to replicate any hotfixes or updates performed on the production environment on the developer environment.

Do not take shortcuts when it comes to setting up a development environment.

Q: Can you provide an example of when a straight .NET development is more appropriate than SharePoint .NET?

A: One size does not fit all. At times a .NET development can be more appropriate than SharePoint development. You will have to ask yourself, "What are my requirements?", "How many of those requirements can SharePoint out of the box (OOTB) meet?", and "How much effort is included in custom developing the requirements that SharePoint does not natively meet?". The last and most likely the most important question you should ask yourself is, What do I gain from implementing this in SharePoint?

When looking to build a solution you first have to understand the functionality that is required. There are some things that SharePoint does not do well natively and a considerable amount of development will be necessary to achieve the desired results. It might feel like fitting a square peg into a round hole at times. One example is when organizations want to implement a site with the e-commerce functionality. Although it is possible with SharePoint development, there may be other ways to leverage existing .NET solutions on the market. SharePoint does not provide e-commerce features that a SharePoint developer can leverage. In the end, a SharePoint developer will be building all of the components and functionality manually and trying to make them work within SharePoint. If there are no SharePoint features that can be leveraged it defeats the purpose of using SharePoint, and .NET development might be a better option.

At times SharePoint is simply not required and you will have to evaluate the advantages of using SharePoint to build a business case.

 This decision should not be made by a developer, for obvious reasons. But this often happens if the developer is the only technical person in a department.

One advantage to using SharePoint is that the amount of custom development might be less than building a .NET application from scratch. The caveat is that with SharePoint Development you always have to factor in the cost of SharePoint licenses, server licenses, the resources to manage SharePoint, and the built-in customizations. When you factor it all in, a .NET application might be a better candidate for development.

Q: What do I need to know to get started in SharePoint development?

A: There are three things you need to know as a SharePoint developer. They are as follows:

.NET development

Getting started in .NET development requires knowledge of Visual Studio 2010, knowledge of programming languages such as C#/VB.NET, object-oriented programming, and ASP.NET pages (including ASP.NET page lifecycle, code-behind, controls, and HTML markup). Having a solid understanding of these principles allows the developer to move to the next stage of SharePoint development, which is to understand SharePoint as a platform.

How SharePoint features function within the platform

SharePoint packages and deploys every customization as a feature and this knowledge is essential for developers so they can create, deploy, and manage these SharePoint custom features. If for example, a developer is required to develop the functionality for end users to create a marketing library and a marketing calendar, the developer might create a custom "marketing" feature to achieve the functionality. Features are end user accessible and can be activated and deactivated by end users. The custom "marketing" features would create or delete the marketing library and calendar on activation and deactivation. This simplistic scenario nicely highlights the function of SharePoint features.

How to deploy customizations

SharePoint deploys every feature as a web solution package (WSP). WSPs typically consist of multiple features and in turn, multiple customizations. It is possible to deploy customizations without WSPs but it is not recommended and is not the best practice. The basic function of a WSP is to package customizations and deploy them on the SharePoint server. Instead of manually copying files to specific locations on a SharePoint Server, a WSP will specify where they should be copied on the SharePoint Server. WSPs are installed on the SharePoint Server via a command-line tool called PowerShell. Once installed on SharePoint, they can be deployed via command line or the SharePoint user interface. On deployment, SharePoint will unpack all the content packaged by the WSP, and install files to the appropriate location.

Understanding these three areas will get a developer started in SharePoint development. These basics will help develop web parts, workflows, and other components for SharePoint.

Q: What technical environment do I need to get started with SharePoint development?

A: SharePoint development requires development tools such as Visual Studio and SharePoint Designer to be on all the environments. Yes, that means Development, User Acceptance Testing, and Production environments. Visual Studio will need to be deployed on Production, so code can be deployed and perhaps tested.

There are two main virtualization options, **Hyper-V** and **VMWare**. The main reason a virtualized environment is necessary with SharePoint development is because development requires a SharePoint Server environment. Developers are used to workstations employing Windows XP/Windows Vista/Windows 7 to develop for .NET projects. It is possible to use a workstation for SharePoint development but that will require the installation of a SharePoint Server on the developer's workstation. This approach has significant drawbacks. When a server is installed locally, its constant running can decrease performance of the overall workstation. For this reason, a virtualized environment is usually the preferred approach.

Another virtualization environment that you could consider is VirtualBox. This software is available for free at `https://www.virtualbox.org/`.

Windows Server 2008 is required in order to run Hyper-V virtual machines. Hyper-V only runs on Windows Server 2008 so it's not possible to run a Hyper-V from Windows XP or Windows 7. This alone can deter most from choosing Hyper-V.

Both virtual environments allow you to take snapshots so that you can always save the state of the virtual environment and revert to it if you choose. The virtual environment allows the developer to develop for SharePoint without having to install SharePoint on his/her workstation. Virtual environments allow the installation of Windows Server 2008 or any other operating system, running and stopping that environment as required. Know that SharePoint requires a certain amount of memory and disk space, which can influence where you run your virtual machines. If you are running the virtual machine from a developer workstation, the workstation needs to have enough memory and disk space to accommodate it. Many developers prefer VMWare because of the portability of virtual machines. VMWare allows developers to run the virtual environment on any operating system or workstation, even on an Apple computer.

Once the virtualized environment has been chosen you will need to install SharePoint Server and all the development tools on that virtual machine. Take the time to investigate how you want your development environment set up. You should always try to create a development environment that simulates the production environment you are developing for. This could mean that you update the server with the appropriate service packs and server updates and use the same server configurations and security. Install the same SharePoint Server version on your development environment that you have installed in production.

The main tool for development that should be installed on your development environment is Visual Studio 2010. Most developers are already using Visual Studio 2010 but have been unable to create any SharePoint customizations because Visual Studio does not recognize that a local SharePoint Server has been installed. Even though there are several add-ons that can be installed for Visual Studio for SharePoint development, they are not required for SharePoint development. As a developer, most of the customizations you will develop can be done with Visual Studio 2010. There might be situations, however, where you will need other tools. SharePoint Designer 2010, InfoPath 2010, Visio 2010, and Office 2010 will soon become part of your development process.

Q: Do developers ever resist the SharePoint developer route?

A: A weird question you may think, but this happens all the time and there is a pure school of developers that are anti-SharePoint. There are three distinct reasons for the resistance:

SharePoint development is not considered professional development

Many developers look down on SharePoint development for several reasons. SharePoint development lacks some of the basic development standards. Many developers complain that it lacks a unit-testing story. A common complaint among developers is that it is difficult to work with and deploy. Part of that difficulty is the complexity in development environments. Developers also cannot see the benefit of SharePoint development and how it helps them in their development tasks.

Developers do not want to work within a product

To some developers working within a product framework can feel restrictive and perhaps not as malleable as the current new technologies that we've come to know and love. It can feel somewhat "behind the times". SharePoint tools can seem more like configuration rather than development. This is a reality of the product and is a valid resistance. Development must become a broader definition than just writing code, it must become more solution focused.

Most developers do not want to be end user focused

Developers are wired differently than say, business analysts (just look at their desks). They are technical and their level of expertise is hyper-focused. They want to write code and they want that code appreciated. End users don't usually provide this kind of affirmation. However, they may not have the skill set to apply what will essentially benefit the end user.

Developers want to be good at what they do and that means efficiency. It can be difficult for developers to put themselves in the shoes of the end user because an end user usually doesn't see all the things "under the hood". SharePoint developers need to place themselves in the shoes of the end user throughout the development process and sometimes that means sacrificing the cool things that can be done with raw code and implementing the best strategies for the end user. This doesn't necessarily mean they reject being end user focused, but rather they need user interface skills, user acceptance, and managing expectation skills. Although the project management will usually be coordinating this with the developer, this form of communication to the project manager is essential.

Funny you should say that...

This section explains some typical follow-up questions you may have in bringing the developer into the SharePoint development world.

Q: How do I know that my developers just do not have the SharePoint knowledge?

A: In a world where everyone is an expert and senior developer this can be a challenge.

A by-product of being a beginner as a SharePoint Developer is that they tend to make several classic mistakes. A seasoned SharePoint developer will immediately pick up on the mistakes and also understand that with experience the beginning developer will understand how to correct those mistakes. There are other mistakes that a SharePoint developer with a lack of understanding of SharePoint may make.

- **Not really SharePoint development**: I witnessed a project where a developer built a custom .NET application and made it viewable within a SharePoint page. This functionality is easily achieved using an out of the box web part (page viewer web part) that allows an end user to configure the web part to point to a URL. The web part will then display the site as if it natively lives inside of SharePoint within a page. This is clearly not SharePoint development or successful integration. There was no need for SharePoint in that particular example and it was clear that the developer lacked knowledge to correctly leverage SharePoint. Ask, "Is SharePoint necessary in your architected solution?". If the answer is no, that might be an indication that the developer has failed to understand SharePoint development. It could also mean that SharePoint is not really necessary and the bigger question is, "Are you using SharePoint in the correct scenario?".

- **Reinventing the wheel**: Developers naturally want to build. They have a tendency to try to re-invent the wheel. Developers try to build functionality that is already available or fail to leverage existing SharePoint functionality. They have failed to understand that there are many built-in features that a developer can use. They do this because they simply don't understand SharePoint as a platform but maybe more importantly fail to understand the purpose of using SharePoint altogether. If you find a developer recreating SharePoint functionality such as simple workflows, e-mail notifications, authentication, or security it might be a sign that the developer has missed the concept of SharePoint development.

- **Manual deployments**: When a developer is manually moving files to servers to deploy customizations it is a good indicator that they don't have the SharePoint knowledge in deployment. Developers are used to deploying web applications by copying files to a server directory. In SharePoint development, Web Solution Packages (WSP) are used to standardize deployment. SharePoint will take care of deploying all packaged files to the appropriate locations on the server. Files that have been edited manually on the server can become a real nightmare to manage. For this reason and many more, SharePoint has implemented a standard deployment process. If a developer fails to see the benefit and take advantage of the standard deployment processes, he/she has clearly missed the point of SharePoint development.

The hardest part is making the distinction between mistakes that stem from being a beginning SharePoint developer or from not understanding SharePoint altogether. Understanding the boundaries, the advantages, and the processes of SharePoint development are a great indicator of sufficient knowledge of SharePoint.

This chapter has explained that SharePoint is built using the .NET Framework that allows you to build and integrate .NET components within the platform. So SharePoint is a .NET web application.

Most web applications will need the following:

- Security
- Data Repository
- Reporting
- Business Process automation/Workflows
- User interfaces
- Collaboration
- Administration

The SharePoint platform provides the previously described features without writing a line of code. This knowledge is key to .NET development leveraging the SharePoint environment.

Q: Does a SharePoint developer need better than normal communication skills?

A: There is no question that a SharePoint developer needs above average communication skills. A SharePoint developer will focus on the following four specific areas that require a higher level of communication than that employed by the average developer:

- **Requirements gathering**: Most organizations try to implement SharePoint with out of the box functionality, but further exploration of requirements is necessary in order to determine if custom work is involved. Therefore, a developer will need to take part in the requirements gathering meetings and provide input and direction. Sometimes the luxury of a project manager is not available.

- **Technical and business decision making**: An organization may be better able to make decisions based on the recommendations and expertise of the SharePoint developer. A developer will need to be able to communicate with non-technical decision makers and discuss pros and cons, feasibility of the requirements, budget, and timelines.

- **Training**: Not all SharePoint developers are involved in training, but in smaller organizations a developer might find himself/herself in more of a teacher position. He/she may be asked to put together training manuals, governance plans, administrative manuals, and to conduct training sessions. Success as a trainer, educator, or writer requires better communication on a wider scale than communicating solely with those at a similar technical level. You must be accessible to more audiences.

- **End-to-end delivery**: SharePoint developers deliver solutions from conception to the final deployment to a production environment. Through these many phases of SharePoint implementation, the developer will be involved with many people with different motivations and different learning strategies. One must be a superior communicator with a keen ability to understand his/her audience.

Digging deeper

Now you may have a SharePoint development project on the project plan horizon and you are thinking how to introduce the development team to SharePoint. This section answers some of your questions.

Q: How can I learn SharePoint development as fast as possible?

A: There are many ways to learn SharePoint development very quickly. There are many books in the market that can prove to be great learning resources. One way to learn SharePoint development quickly is to become connected to the SharePoint community. The community involves local User Groups, Social media (Twitter), and public forums. There are also online training companies that provide self-pace programs.

Find a user group

There are thousands of user groups all over North America and around the world. They are usually led by SharePoint MVPs and supported by Microsoft. The format is quite relaxed and generally consists of a monthly event. Events usually consist of a presentation from a local or remote speaker. Presentation topics can be very informative and introduce you to technical topics that can prove beneficial. Although presentations are great, one of the best part of the user groups is that you get a chance to meet other SharePoint developers in your area. Find a user group near you on MSDN (`http://msdn.microsoft.com/en-ca/aa974219`). If you cannot find a user group near you, consider starting one. You do not have to be a SharePoint expert in order to start a user group.

Connect through social media

If you want to know what other developers are working on, subscribe to their blog roll or follow them on Twitter. Twitter might be the best way to connect with other SharePoint developers and find out when new blog posts or other SharePoint material is being published on the Internet.

Developers to follow on twitter:

- Sahil Malik
- Bil Simser
- Rob Windsor
- Mosslover
- @redmondhockey
- @chrisO_brien

Some of the notable SharePoint experts to follow beyond development are:

- @jthake
- @joeloleson
- @harbars
- @mosslover
- @kkhipple
- @sharepointbuzz

Two SharePoint-related hashtags are:

- #SharePoint
- #SPhelp

Connecting to experts can be beneficial not only because of the content they produce but also to connect to other notable experts they follow. Make sure to subscribe or bookmark their blogs; this way you can learn from their informative blogs.

Forums

Forums are a great way to request help on and research issues that you might encounter. They tend to become the first resource you turn to when researching an issue you are experiencing. The most popular forums are:

- MSDN/Technet: `http://social. technet. microsoft. com/Forums/en-US/category/sharepoint2010`
- StackOverflow: `http://stackoverflow.com`
- StackExchange: `http://stackexchange.com`
- Meta StackOverflow: `http://meta.stackoverflow.com)`

Personally, it took some of the authors about a year to really start getting a grasp on SharePoint development. They were dedicated and involved in SharePoint development projects as well as in configuring and installing SharePoint. This gave them an opportunity to learn the product and understand what needed to be customized and what could be used out of the box. They were also working in teams where fellow team members could mentor them. It takes some time and experience to become a great SharePoint developer and it takes longer if a developer is not fully dedicated to SharePoint projects. Many organizations have developers working on several projects, many that are not SharePoint, and it can be quite difficult to overcome the learning curve when that happens.

Q: What SharePoint books do you recommend for learning development?

A: There are several books I would recommend to a beginner diving into SharePoint. It would likely be beneficial to read a book that describes what SharePoint is and its core functionality. The book, *Microsoft SharePoint 2010 End User Guide: Business Performance Enhancement*, gives a good overview of product features and limitations. If you are the type of person who likes to understand how the whole works before diving into specifics, reading this book might be the best place to start.

For development, *Microsoft SharePoint 2010 Development with Visual Studio 2010 Expert Cookbook* can provide you with code samples and tutorials to get started. The *SharePoint Development Unleashed* series of books is quite informative and provides many code samples and tutorials as well. As a beginning SharePoint developer the best book is a reference you can come back to when you are developing similar customizations. When you start development, you will be concerned with how to instantiate SharePoint objects, and how to create lists and document libraries programmatically. Basically, you will be focused on recreating functionality that you can perform out of the box and will be looking for ways to automate tasks.

Wrox books on Development and Administration are excellent but they are a bit different. They do a great job of teaching how-to but they provide a lot of overview as well. To get the most from them one must be ready to dive deeper into the overall functionality of SharePoint. Wrox administration books are very informative because of the overview they provide. As a developer matures, they will understand the need to learn configuration to allow them to be better SharePoint developers. The more knowledgeable a developer is with administration the better they can understand the boundaries of the product and where custom development can enhance the platform.

The last book I recommend for beginners is *Real World SharePoint 2010*. It will give you an overview of a lot of the SharePoint 2010 product with great step-by-step instructions around configuration and solutions. As a beginner, you will get instructions on creating your own complete development environment. This will include configuring DNS, Active Directory, SQL Server, complete SharePoint installation with FAST Search, and User Profiles. It is a great start to understanding how all these pieces fit together. Each chapter is quite informative and practical. If you get to a point where you want to jump into reporting services, branding, and other SharePoint features and capabilities, this book would likely be a great start.

Summary

SharePoint development is a large topic of discussion that involves many technologies and a wide array of skills. In this chapter, we discussed issues from the differences between .NET and SharePoint development, to the challenges and roadblocks, to the best ways to learn SharePoint development. Although we have only begun to scratch the surface on SharePoint development hopefully you have understood the issues and challenges of transforming a developer into a SharePoint Solution Architect rock star.

7
Growing SharePoint Capacity and Meeting Staffing Resource Needs

In the previous chapters, we discussed SharePoint strategy, SharePoint projects, and governance approaches. Now imagine that you are sitting at your desk and you want to unleash SharePoint into the veins of the organization. This chapter discusses how to grow SharePoint capacity, build and acquire skills sets needed, and allow the reader to understand some of the hidden costs of a SharePoint deployment, and how to assess success after the first year of deployment.

Q: What are the minimal SharePoint deployment and technical skill set I can get away with?

A: Assuming that this is an on-premise installation, the minimal deployment would be SharePoint 2010 Foundation. It already resides on Windows 2008 servers and can be installed for no additional cost. The **Content Database** and all other services can reside on that one server. The caveat is future-proofing for size, traffic, and lack of features available on Standard and Enterprise Editions.

A SharePoint Foundation deployment would be perfect for smaller operations (both in number of users and overall size of content) or as a Proof of Concept. It allows you to introduce the platform and gives organizations the opportunity to begin with core SharePoint collaboration and out of the box approval workflows.

Be wary of the growth of multiple deployments of individual SharePoint Foundation installations within your organization. Linking them together eventually will require a great deal of custom configuring and cost more than the money saved on not having purchased licenses, planned an architecture and managed a deployment. Attempts to reengineer SharePoint may come back to haunt you when trying to make adjustments to the architecture.

There are feature workarounds, for example pages can be coded to mimic some Standard and Enterprise features, but again is the time and cost of building and maintaining these workarounds going to be greater than the time and cost of having the Out of the Box solutions in place?

A common example of this workaround happens when Foundation is deployed as an Internet-facing site. To effectively use SharePoint for web pages you would need to have the publishing features that will be available in the Standard Edition. These features allow you to build, edit, and post content quickly through web parts.

Because publishing features are not present in Foundation, you could technically open up pages and CSS styles on the background via SharePoint Designer. To include these features would require hardcoding and that takes a high-level skill set. Since rapid publishing features are not available in SharePoint Foundation, the person responsible for the site would have to make any changes by hand coding. So a double loss is possible, one being the loss of time when a highly skilled member of staff would have to constantly make changes to the site and the other being the recovery time that would add up if an under-skilled staff member makes the slightest mistake! If your organization still wants to proceed with a Proof of Concept and sees the need to do so with Standard and Enterprise features there is a way to do so without having to acquire production SharePoint licenses.

If your organization has the **Visual Studio Premium** or **Ultimate** level MSDN subscription, then you possess a version of SharePoint that can be used for development and testing purposes only. Once a deployment is moved to production you will be responsible for the correct licensing in accordance with your server environment and **Client Access License (CAL)** guides based on number of users.

Assuming that this is an on-premise installation, a System Administrator could handle all the duties of installation and maintenance. This person, in short, would be in charge of all aspects from the very technical administration of the server and database environment including backup and security to the creation of site collections, adding/deleting users, and having to respond to end-user needs such as help desk functions and training.

The immediate drawback to this role of being the SharePoint person would be the organizational expectations of this person's time and the business-critical aspects that SharePoint would assume. For example, if critical records are stored in SharePoint, their care and planned recovery would need to be documented. Should an event occur, then this person may be in charge of too much of the entire IT structure and making the recovery of the single item of content could become a much delayed task.

The best plan of attack is to create a Governance Plan/Policies Document and committee (in which a System Administrator would be involved) to keep a watchful eye on your SharePoint deployment. The best way to approach filling roles for this committee is to divide and assign staff into groups such as Operations, Support, Development, and Business Goals.

Ideally if SharePoint is a major part of the organization's strategy then only having an IT admin resource could present some drawbacks. Normally these IT admins are operationally driven and may execute their task in that fashion. This could be very cut and dry. If their task is to install and configure a system they may do that in the quickest manner so as to get the project completed as soon as possible.

This type of execution would not take into consideration the actual business needs or objectives that SharePoint features could address, making this a potential failure before it even had a chance. Lack of communication and true goal setting with the business user section of your organization would ensure this. SharePoint is many things to many people but its true mission is to be a Platform for the end/power user community.

 If your SharePoint deployment does not included business-level goals and communication when setting strategy, the likely outcome is that SharePoint becomes "just another other tool to learn" for your staff that does not recognize organizational needs and therefore will not enable staff to realize their potential. In short, why not let your organization's business goals be the driving force for Solution Architecture?

Q: What would be the typical SharePoint skill sets needed for different company sizes?

A: In order to understand what skill sets are needed, organizations must first make sure that a few things are in place. Two of the most important things for any organization, big or small, are to first architect a scalable foundation and plan for administrative efforts to maintain SharePoint. The first budget allocations must include these in order to have a firm foundation from which to grow.

The next step is to identify someone with the ability to advocate and promote SharePoint's usage in the organization. This role should be easy to find from within because often enough this is not an IT person but a business power user who has a deep knowledge of your business and is passionate about how SharePoint's feature sets can improve efficiency.

While that may sound easy enough you still need to fill IT-based roles. You may still not be familiar with the current IT industry title to skill sets matrix. So in that case it is better to start asking yourself who in the organization will do the following:

- Install it
- Support it
- Recover it
- Fix it
- Provide access
- Expand on the initial deployment
- Know when to call in consulting services
- Help end users adopt it

Once you have drawn up this list you may very well find that one person may cover more than one of these functions and in some cases all of them. As mentioned earlier, smaller SharePoint Foundation deployments can be carried out by one individual. Organizations that have greater content and staff resources can permit themselves to staff more personnel to keep SharePoint running. For organizations of 100-1000 staff members, the following positions or their combinations will more than likely be needed:

- **System Administrator**: The System Administrator would typically be in charge of the acquisition, installation, and maintenance of the hardware infrastructure as well as day-to-day operation support, review existing infrastructure setup, develop best practices, create operation guidelines, install operating-system updates/service packs, and maintain logs.
- **SharePoint Farm Administrator**: The SharePoint Farm Administrator is responsible for global portal configuration, policies, procedures, and portal vision, application management, search administration, workflow management, backup and restore, data configuration, and content deployment.
- **SQL Administrator**: The SQL Administrator restores, backs up, and maintains the SQL environment as well as any security and performance tuning.

- **Enterprise Site Collections Administrator**: The Enterprise Site Collections Administrator maintains search settings, site-collection usage reports, storage-space allocation, site-collection features, site hierarchy, site-usage reports, workflows, and Master page layouts. Also in many cases they take on Level 1 and Level 2 support.

- **Active Directory Resources**: Active Directory Resources set up the portal Active Directory for authentication and assist in synchronization of SharePoint with Active Directory.

Once these roles are in place and there have been good returns on the Proof of Concept or Pilot program then the time has come to improve and customize SharePoint for a production-deployment, in other words time to build upon SharePoint's capabilities.

For organizations greater than 1000 members in staff, this may first necessitate increasing the layers of the positions described earlier; it also will certainly mean adding on development based skill sets such as the following positions:

- **Developers** to build upon existing custom look and feel, modify templates, build new web parts, and write ASP.NET code

- **Product and Program Management** that is responsible for business advocacy and resources, delivering solutions and advocacy to satisfied stakeholders

- **SharePoint Branding Designer** who enhances the Out of the Box User Interface and usability, creates and change images, CSS, master pages, and layouts

Q: How easy is it to train in-house technical staff on SharePoint?

A: When it comes to training staff, there are many options. Your training need, whether it is for administrators, developers, or power users, can all be addressed by classroom training. Many established training companies have existing courses and use subject matter experts as contractors. This may be effective for end-user training and some power-user training that requires more hands-on time and knowledge procedural execution. If you have an internal training team, they may purchase pre-packaged training but they would then need the necessary time to gain mastery of the content.

For more advanced "real-world" situational administrator and developer training, these companies may fall short of expectations due to their dependence on lab-related course material. Therefore it may be better to find a company that specializes in more advanced areas of SharePoint. These companies will have subject matter experts that not only train but also carry out implementations. Typically this type of SharePoint subject matter expert is closely involved in course creation and therefore the day-to-day expectations of platform itself.

Another option if you happen to use consultants to deploy SharePoint is to make sure to allocate their time to provide training. They may not be classic trainers but they will have knowledge about your business use and needs. In this case, it is not so much training as it is a complete knowledge transfer at handoff. It goes without saying that the consultants will know your SharePoint solution intimately. Things to be gained by this approach are that your staff will learn about their solution from an execution point of view.

The drawback is that they may not gain foundational SharePoint concepts that will be needed once the occasion to extend the existing configuration presents itself.

Whatever choice (or combination of them) you decide upon, make sure that training needs and strategy are discussed and documented when your Governance plan is created.

Q: What kind of training resources are available?

A: Training new staff or increasing current staff's skill sets in SharePoint should also be considered when forming a strategy. Realistically speaking receiving a complete and comprehensive end-to-end training in SharePoint is close to impossible for any one person to complete. The simple reason is that there is simply too much to learn in order to understand all there is to know about this platform. Beginning with a Proof of Concept and keeping it as a Sandbox environment will allow staff to have an area where they can build skills in order to become familiar with the platform and not impact production environments. This approach is an excellent idea.

There are a number of training services and Microsoft Partners who offer courses for all the different SharePoint roles: Administration, Developer, End User, Power End User, Site Collection Administrator, and so on. Typically these providers offer boot camp-style courses that last anywhere from two to five days. There are also written and web-based courses that you can purchase, which can be given to internal training staff to either teach or post to learning management portals.

Another alternative is to have your staff achieve Microsoft Certification in SharePoint. There are three paths to certification and they are broken down into three main groups:

- Power User
- Administrator
- Developer

Exam 77-886 Microsoft Office Specialist: SharePoint 2010

The audience for this exam according to Microsoft is "users who provide structure for information, extend out of the box site features, solve business problems through composite applications, and facilitate collaboration with other site users."

By passing this exam you gain Microsoft Office Specialist (MOS): SharePoint 2010 status.

Exam 70-667 Microsoft SharePoint 2010, Configuration

The audience for this exam according to Microsoft "typically has more than one year of experience configuring SharePoint and related technologies, including Internet Information Services (IIS), Windows Server 2008, and Active Directory, and networking infrastructure services."

By passing this exam you:

- Gain MCTS—Microsoft Certified Technology Specialist status
- Gain MCP—Microsoft Certified Professional status
- Passing 70-667 is a credit towards MCITP—Microsoft Certified IT Professional

Exam 70-668 SharePoint 2010, Configuration

The audience for this exam according to Microsoft should be able to "design and deploy SharePoint online and on-premise SharePoint 2010 SP1 infrastructures. These candidates might be senior administrators who act as the technical lead over a team of administrators. Candidates should have a minimum of two years of experience administering, deploying, managing, monitoring, upgrading, migrating, and designing SharePoint solutions."

If 70-667 and 70-668 are successfully completed, candidates gain MCITP—Microsoft Certified IT Professional status.

Exam 70-543 SharePoint 2010, Application Development

The audience for this exam, according to Microsoft are candidates that should be able "to write code that extends SharePoint 2010, add and support code to an existing project, write code for and test custom features in a SharePoint solution such as a Visual Web Part or Event Receiver, and implement a solution designed by lead SharePoint Developer."

By passing this exam you:

- Gain MCTS — Microsoft Certified Technology Specialist status
- Gain MCP — Microsoft Certified Professional status
- 70-573 is a credit towards MCPD — Microsoft Certified Professional Developer

Exam 70-576 Designing and Developing Microsoft SharePoint 2010 Applications

The audience for this exam according to Microsoft candidates are "responsible for designing custom code for projects that are deployed to SharePoint servers. This includes technology selection across the many ways to build code in SharePoint, ensuring the team development environment is configured, creating a strategy for code deployment, versioning, configuration, or structure."

If 70-543 and 70-576 are successfully completed, candidates gain MCPD Microsoft Certified Professional Developer status.

The advantage using this training path is that your staff is not obligated to pay for training classes. There are published training plans by Microsoft that recommend not only formal courses but also books and articles that are geared towards each certification exam. The knowledge base in these exam books and articles covers far more than is necessary to pass the exams and therefore offers a more complete learning path to SharePoint while at the same time motivating staff to pass a recognized professional certification.

Funny you should say that...

This section explains some typical follow up questions you may have once you start to think about how to grow your SharePoint capacity.

Q: Should I listen to recruiters on job descriptions?

A: Competent SharePoint skills are hard to find. It is not currently taught in universities. If a Business or Computer Science graduate finds his or her way to an entry-level position there is a possibility that the employer has SharePoint and then if the organization has a developed strategy they have the possibility to gain experience. Alternatively if the employees are permitted, they can embark on a self-training regimen but this would be a time consuming effort (given the platform nature of the product) even if they had no other obligations.

Therefore it makes sense to go to the market place for talent. Currently SharePoint skills are at a premium. Many qualified SharePoint professionals are currently engaged and would need to be compensated accordingly to make a move.

Recruiters that do not possess specialization and knowledge of SharePoint often have job requisitions that are either over extending or do not fully describe what is needed. The most popular example of this over extending job title that you will see is a SharePoint Developer. The job description for this role is often borrowed and refreshed with SharePoint skill buzz words from those of .NET developers. The following is an example of a recent job description sent by a recruiter:

SharePoint Developer:

- Five year's experience in SharePoint 2010
- Developing web parts, and deploying third-party solutions
- Demonstrated knowledge of Central Administration
- Active Directory authentication, Search and integration with other Microsoft products including Exchange, Project Server, Outlook, and so on
- Ability to perform basic SQL Server administration including database creation, backup, and cloning
- Excellent troubleshooting and problem resolution skills
- Knowledge of Service Oriented Architecture (SOA) and web services
- Ability to manage multiple tasks, work in a team environment, understand and be responsive to project needs, and work under tight deadlines
- Five plus years of technical lead experience in one or more of the following roles:
  - Web Services Development
  - Data Access Development
  - Mobile Application Development

- ° Security
- ° Application integration
- ° Testing and Deployment
- ° User Interface Design

Preferred requirements:

- Microsoft Certification
- You will have demonstrated strong knowledge and advanced proficiency in the following:
  - ° SharePoint 2010
  - ° Commerce Server
  - ° Content Management Server
  - ° BizTalk Server

The previous job description is a classic example of the recruiter realizing that your organization has multiple technologies and trying to find a candidate that has this skill set. The reality is that practically no one has this skill set and if they do, they are probably a generalist in the subject matters, rather than a specialist.

The candidates that apply to the above job description are technology guys, and if this is your first SharePoint project, for you to utilize their skill set, you will need development and testing environments, and development tools. Does this SharePoint project warrant this skill set to be used?

Other wrong factors with this job description are: SharePoint 2010 was available to some in late 2009 and yet the job description asks for five years' experience. The math does not add up (as of the printing/publication of this book). Also take into consideration that the highly regarded development aspect is mentioned only fractionally compared to the trend of bullets that place a much larger emphasis on administrative aspects.

Many recruiters believe that this type of "builder" is the one position that can do it all. This may not be the role that is needed if you are starting out with SharePoint. By using this developer who can build everything, you are risking skipping over the need for administrative skill sets that can configure "to the max". That is more important when maintaining SharePoint. So it is recommended that you assess the recruiter's past performance in placing SharePoint professionals.

Q: What are the hidden costs of SharePoint?

A: A common assumption is that SharePoint is as easy as running the install and turning it over to your staff to collaborate and nothing else should be considered besides licensing and staffing. While these two do need to be accounted for, there are other aspects that organizations need to incorporate into their plans, strategy, and budgets.

SharePoint Backup, **Content Migration**, and **Virus Checking** can all be considered hidden costs to those not familiar with the platform. As mentioned before in this book there is a healthy ecosystem of third-party products and services available to address these hidden cost areas.

SharePoint is database driven, so backup is as easy as just recovering the database, right? While that is true to a certain extent you will need to look (again) if you have the staff that possesses the high-level of SharePoint knowledge that spans all the little quirks and "gotchas" that this approach entails. Even with this knowledge in place is it worth the time and effort to carry out such a process that may be streamlined by a third-party service or product? That just covers the backup part of the equation; now ask yourself what are the recovery times that are acceptable. Once you have a deployment in place, make sure to take note on how long it took. Are you prepared to reinvest in similar time frames to manually rebuild? After you begin tallying up the potential totals then third-party backup and recovery make perfect sense.

The same scenario applies to migration as well. Moving an entire organization's content from one system to SharePoint is going to take a fair amount of time. Do you have the time to allow the uploading or copying of hundreds of GBs when a product could do it in half to a quarter of the time with metadata in place? Yes, manually moving files would also need to account for adding metadata once files are in SharePoint.

The question in this case is how much content there is to move. If a SharePoint project is meant to be a "line in the sand" where only new content goes in, then this time and cost do not need to be applied. In that case the amount of content does not justify the cost of the additional tool.

As for Virus checking, out of the box protection options are certainly available, but just as in the personal computing space, there are services that go above and beyond. Within SharePoint products and services ecosystem, there are products that have been developed with the advantage of SharePoint knowledge bases that dealt with many of the problems that you may encounter.

While you may have enough space in your content database, other hidden costs may be the additional need for servers and even more licensing. An example that comes to mind are any servers dedicated for Disaster Recovery. These should be put in place to take over in case the production environment fails.

I am sure you are asking yourself "Apart from Disaster Recovery why would you need more servers?" The easiest explanation is that some of the larger applications in SharePoint 2010 begin to take on a life of their own and that need may not be for more size (space) but actual processor strength (performance). Search functionality usually is the first child to leave the house because as content and user population grow it will need more muscle in order to return quicker results. If you are using any Business Intelligence features, you may find that Enterprise SQL licensing needs to be in place in order to handle all the SQL instances that need to be present within your farm as well as speed of data processing.

Another example where performance is a key issue is in regards to physical distance within the organization. If you have users who are spread out nationally or internationally it may make more sense (for performance and compliance) to have say, European-based teams closer to European-based server farms and only use the central farm when accessing central corporate applications and content.

Other hidden SharePoint costs are SharePoint activities working with existing business processes and making these processes more efficient. This activity may not see immediate benefits and in some cases the business value of migrating a process to SharePoint may not be justified. This is why prioritizing initiatives, which was discussed in *Chapter 1, Defining a SharePoint IT Strategy*, is so important.

Q: Is there a good approach when using SharePoint for a "charge back" model to the business?

A: In the past, IT costs were incurred by a centralized department in an organization and it was seen as petty to charge the marketing department extra because their inboxes were clogged with large PowerPoint attachments. These costs are simply treated as corporate overhead, a straightforward, simple accounting strategy for cost allocation.

Now with the increased adoption of private cloud infrastructures, SaaS, PaaS and SOA, it has become easier to measure usage/consumption and associated allocation costs and a chargeback strategy is now possible for costs incurred. This shift in cost-allocation turns internal IT organization into a service provider and encourages users to treat IT services as they would treat any other utility.

So the answer to this question is that it depends on the specifications of each deployment and the maturity of your SharePoint farm, your IT department, and the organization as a whole. Based upon legal/regulatory requirements and barriers of entry, organizations may fall into one of these two categories:

- **Lock-in**: In these organizations, IT is the sole service provider for collaboration services and business units have to go through IT for all their collaboration needs.

- **Competitive**: In these organizations, IT competes with other external service providers. Business units can write a check to an outside collaboration provider as easily as they can for IT. If your organization falls into this category, then some internal collaboration selling may be required and if SharePoint is unknown, this could be a challenge for buy-in. With this category, user adoption and training are keys to obtain business value.

A chargeback strategy could include any of the following, either alone or as a combination:

- **Charge per site**: Business units are charged based upon the total number of sites they have; discourages the creation of subsites.

- **Charge per user**: Business units are charged based upon the number of users; encourages adoption since you are paying for it anyway; promotes system abuse; unfair cost burden. This approach is difficult to measure and is not recommended.

- **Charge per GB**: Business units are charged based upon storage used by their sites; encourages users to move content to other storage systems; fair cost burden; discourages adoption for new users who are comfortable with file shares and e-mail.

Q: Is it worth purchasing a Microsoft Enterprise License Agreement?

A: Making the decision to move from Foundation to Standard and/or Enterprise rides solely on the necessity for feature sets that each has to offer and of course the return on investment that those would bring.

One of the main distinguishing features of 2010 Enterprise Licensing is the inclusion of Business Intelligence (BI). Microsoft's 2010 BI stack (that includes SharePoint and SQL offerings) is highly regarded and is placed in the Gartner's Leader Quadrant for Business Intelligence. BI is the aggregating, analyzing, storing, and reporting on organizational data from different sources in order to make informed business decisions.

SharePoint Enterprise 2010 features offer the capability to create interactive business dashboards that assemble and display business information through built-in web parts, key performance indicators (KPIs), Excel spreadsheets, data-receiving Visio diagrams, PowerPivot, Microsoft SQL Server Reporting Services reports, or various business data connectivity that can assemble information residing in server-side LOB applications.

SharePoint 2010 Enterprise features also include capacity to create and deploy rich client browser-based forms used to gather data when the Microsoft application InfoPath is installed widely in the organization. Users can fill out forms in a Web browser or HTML-enabled mobile device with no download or client components needed.

The advantage is that the end user would not need to have any software to input and submit forms, which were required in previous versions. A similar experience can also be attained using another 2010 Enterprise feature, Access Services capabilities, for the use and distribution of Access databases organization-wide.

2010 Enterprise licensing is also needed in order to use FAST Search in SharePoint. This would be an additional cost and would need to be budgeted. An argument can be made for FAST search if there is a need to have search result returns use contextual sorting based on user profiles, if the overall size of content passes millions of records that need to be searched and returned in seconds, and visual thumbnails are returned that allow you to preview.

Normally the argument here depends largely on the size, amount, and extent of content. The bigger the organization the larger the content and user base will be. Having any filtering advantage in addition will decrease research times.

 SharePoint 2007 Enterprise licensing does offer BI features like KPIs, Excel spreadsheets, and Microsoft SQL Server Reporting Services capabilities though not to the extent of SharePoint 2010.

Digging deeper

Now you are probably thinking and scratching your head about how SharePoint capacity can be grown and where to start. This section provides some direction to your thoughts.

Q: How do I start to grow capacity?

A: The best way is to plan, which is why the strategy roadmap that was discussed is so important, as it prioritizes activities and aligns them to your business needs.

Obviously budget is important, so by aligning a growth path to your business needs, budgets can be allocated accordingly.

Q: What if I can't get budget to grow capacity?

A: Assuming that you have looked at the following:

- Haven't bought top of the line servers
- Servers have been consolidated into a virtualized environment
- Only identified essential SharePoint initiates
- Looked at new training options (training is usually the first item to suffer when there is a budget review)

Review the chargeback model to business units. If this does not work then the reality is that you can't grow SharePoint capacity. Well, not in the near future.

Q: How do I define if SharePoint has been a success after one year?

A: SharePoint is most definably a marathon as opposed to a sprint, so when a year passes, it is time to assess the success based on money spent, resources used, and efficiencies gained. It may be difficult to come up with hard **Return On Investment (ROI)** numbers but that does not mean that success cannot be defined by other factors. SharePoint's early successes should be considered as milestones in a longer journey that should be measured by the stories of success in addition to hard ROI numbers.

A best practice is to use smaller tactical groups for the first SharePoint deployments. That could be a percentage of your entire staff or you can choose certain teams and special projects. These more focused teams will be better able (and motivated) to blend business goals with SharePoint as opposed to a total deployment and a forced change management situation with your entire staff. In return you typically gain the biggest advocates for SharePoint in these groups and they will go on to passionately tell all within the organization "why" and serve as a model of how to best do it.

Once you have these groups selected ask them to track how their performance increased and how they measured it. When that internal case study and reporting is complete, it will be much easier to look at SharePoint objectively and demonstrate how it functions in your organization.

Some of the things you may want to ask to have tracked are:

- How did consolidated collaboration increase performance?
- How much time was saved by having a single version of the truth (one file in one location)?
- How did the leveraging of no-code or no-IT solutions save time?
- How effective were search capabilities?
- How much time was saved by having a single repository for client, corporate, and external data?
- Were any printing costs saved (newsletter blogs instead of printed versions)?
- Was there a decreased use of/need to use other systems that have maintenance costs?

An example could be integrating a department that produces a fair amount of content, that is, **Human Resources (HR)**. A SharePoint HR site could easily put collaboration through its permission paces as HR staff work behind the scenes on content (such as the coming year's benefits documentation) while the rest of the organization only sees the latest (this year's) published version until the new version is ready. A Records Center can be created so that audit-sensitive information (contracts, forms, and so on) is saved as a record. Search would also play a part; staff can execute their own searches for organization policies instead of e-mailing or calling the HR. This in turn would gift HR with more time to be proactive instead of reactive. And we haven't even mentioned a New Hire Work flow that could begin in HR, pass through IT (e-mail setup, and so on), and prepare the hiring manger to get important information completed to only then communicate with the New Hire their reminders for compliance training.

This is a robust example that you could use by simply substituting a few of the variables with other SharePoint features and your organizational setup.

Summary

In this chapter we covered assessing growth and what SharePoint capacity and resources are needed. Growth for SharePoint means many things, so we addressed what skills you need to begin finding internally and externally and what is the status in the market place.

Finding people is only one factor, so we also covered how to train your staff and some of the hidden costs you can identify early on. We also covered when and in what context Enterprise licensing is needed, and finally how to measure success after the first year of deployment.

Growth is always a challenging process. Avoiding the extremes of too much or too little growth can be counter-balanced by having a strategy. Knowing where to begin your plans for this growth strategy will help define what SharePoint success is and can be for your organization.

In the next chapter you will be introduced to how to select and manage your first SharePoint project.

8

Managing your First SharePoint Project

One of the first and most important decisions you make for your team is which project they should undertake. The answer will vary based upon your situation and circumstances. Did you inherit a SharePoint solution from a previous team? Are you the custodian of a relatively stable SharePoint environment whose reach is wide (many departments using it) but shallow (light document management, team sites that are low touch, low value solution and little else)? Are you installing SharePoint for the first time (a "green field approach")?

Regardless of the answers to these questions, the approach you take and the advice this chapter provides assume you want to make a "splash". You've already personally internalized the idea that SharePoint can be transformational and you want to make it transformational within your organization. This chapter provides the answers to the questions you may have and is designed to help you be an instant "hit" and "winner" right out of the gate with your first custom SharePoint solution. These questions range from planning through to execution. How do you decide which project to start with? What's the right mix of complexity versus your team's skills so that you can manage the business users' expectations and overall risk? How do you execute cleanly and learn from mistakes? Lastly, how do you drive the value of the implementation home to the business as a whole?

This chapter is technical in places and may dive too deep for the reader. The technical aspects are necessary so that the answers are clearer to the technical reader.

Let's begin with question number one: What factors should you take into consideration?

Q: What factors should you take into consideration?

A: The success of your organization's future isn't normally in question when you pick your first SharePoint project. Partly because you don't necessarily want to build a mission-critical application using a technology that is new to the organization. However, if you can execute a winning first effort, it will generate buzz and open doors that were previously closed. It may even open up doors you and your colleagues didn't even know existed in the first place. As a result, you need to give greater thought to your first project than you will next time around and should consider the following factors:

Team skill and experience

No matter how great your first project idea is or feels, you need to be able to execute it. Your ability to successfully execute your first project plan depends on your team's core skill sets, business and domain knowledge, expertise, and the scope of the effort. This is nothing new under the sun. *Chapter 6, How to get the .NET Developers on Board quickly?*, discusses skill sets your team *should* have, but more importantly you need to think realistically about the skill set your team actually has today and whether they can be reskilled or you need additional resources. When it comes to team skill and experience, the best guiding concept is to assume they will underperform and not quite meet your expectations. This way you can limit the expectations placed on them and hence reduce the weight on their shoulders and still allow them some room to exceed the expectations. Of course, don't tell that to your team.

Size and scope of the project

A smaller sized project with clear goals is less risky than a larger project with fuzzy goals. There is nothing special about SharePoint when it comes to this. You don't want to pick a project that is too small to add value, but don't bite off more than you can chew.

 With small projects the productivity gains may be done with out of the box functionality and be delivered to the business quicker. This is also an opportunity to begin the learning curve.

Beware: SharePoint can be a breeding ground for grandiose project designs, partly because the way it has often been sold to organizations—It can do anything. After all, there's so much raw material with which you can work out of the box, such as security, smart menus, great support for information architecture, and an almost absurd number of programming options server side, client side, web side, where it just never seems to end. Take care and use caution to keep your ambitions focused.

 There will be plenty of opportunity to climb the SharePoint mountain in the months and years ahead. Don't worry. You can still make a splash without the embarrassment of a public belly flop.

Your customer

Who are your customers and what are their expectations? Are they open and flexible to being part of an experimental process or a pilot program? If you hit more than the expected number of bumps in the road, how will they react? If you are very successful, will they be good champions for your cause and help you take the next big transformational steps with the product? Identify a flexible group of people who won't complain loudly if you fail and who will be good champions for you when you succeed. If you select a customer with these credentials you've hit pay dirt.

Configuration versus customization

SharePoint is extremely easy to customize with code. This platform provides a gamut of opportunities to use Visual Studio for event receivers, custom pages, timer jobs, custom web parts, and so on. On the other hand, the platform provides a significant opportunity to use out of the box features in interesting ways, but which often fall shy of a 100 percent solution. Which path do you follow? The middle road is the best. Limit yourself to one custom web part with a handful of configurable properties. Consider an event receiver to do some intelligent metadata default calculations. Don't create half a dozen web parts with an extensively customized user interface. And most importantly, take advantage of the platform.

Q: Why is a SharePoint first project different to other technologies' first project?

A: Fundamentally, SharePoint isn't really any different from any other projects. The factors you just read about apply equally well to your typical CRM, ERP, or other system rollout. But there are some important differences that you need to understand, if you don't want to end up in the dust bin of SharePoint history along with the many other unfortunate souls who jumped into this world without looking first.

One of the key pitfalls into which too many organizations fall can best be described with the old saying, "familiarity breeds contempt". SharePoint is after all just a .NET technology platform, based on C# and VB.NET, uses SQL Server as a backend, and Internet Information Services (IIS) for content delivery. It is an ASP.NET application at its core. This does not mean that you only need these hard technical skills for a successful SharePoint project. User training, project management, and managing expectations are still the key.

Many organizations jump into the SharePoint world knowing all these facts and with more than passing experience working with all of those components. As a result, you and your team may think: "This SharePoint thing is just another .NET app and as a result, I already know 99 percent of what I need to know to be successful. It's Microsoft after all, a technology vendor that we have been using for years."

Despite these familiar tools, it's vitally important to recognize that many of these routine processes to which you're accustomed, such as XCOPY deployments, client-server development, direct access to SQL via SQL statements and stored procedures, and even relying upon `web.config` edits for application configuration follow different patterns than the traditional ASP.NET development. This isn't to say that your team's ASP.NET knowledge has no value, but you need to take great care here. SharePoint does many things the same way but it does even more things differently, and the only way to really learn that is by getting your hands dirty, making some mistakes and growing your team's expertise step-by-step. Let's examine a real-world example that illustrates this point.

Case Study: The insurance firm

An insurance organization in the New York metro area contracted with a vendor to build a major new piece of business functionality on SharePoint that would enable their non-employee agents to do business via the Web. They selected a vendor with a proven track record of building similar .NET and ASP.NET-based applications. However, the vendor had not worked with SharePoint before. They ended up building a solution riddled with problems. To name three:

- They implemented a custom security interface that stood entirely "outside" of SharePoint. Instead of leveraging out of the box SharePoint security features, they developed a separate module that performed poorly and was bug-ridden and still is to this day.

- They blew up the project schedule with their branding tasks. They didn't understand how SharePoint branding worked. Branding was important in this extranet environment. Although their technical implementation was appropriate for a traditional ASP.NET application, it didn't take a number of core SharePoint facts into account. At the same time, they informed the marketing department that SharePoint could not support the business requirements for branding. They provided bad information and biased the marketing team against SharePoint entirely (not just for branding) for *their entire engagement*.

- They did not understand SharePoint's feature/solution architecture. They used old and familiar XCOPY techniques to deploy the solution from development to QA and finally to production; this is a manual and at times unpredictable process.

To this day, the failures have led to recurring problems that the company continues to manage. The site is unreliable and barely achieves 95 percent uptime. The techniques that the vendor company chose also prevented the site from being upgraded from SharePoint 2007 to SharePoint 2010. The downtime costs to the firm are almost USD $20,000 per hour and the site is unavailable during business hours, which is a major problem for the company.

None of this is to say that the vendor was incompetent. They made a number of architecture and technical decisions on the basis of their understanding of .NET technology. Viewed through that prism, their decisions were entirely logical and appropriate, albeit disastrously wrong. Therefore it is critical to understand the differences in SharePoint and not let your team fall into the same trap.

End-user community

With SharePoint, you typically face a different problem with your end user community. You have probably seen your share of CRM and ERP rollouts over the years. So too has a slice of your end user community. They know what to expect with these and similar business systems. By now some of them have a good amount of hands-on experience with SharePoint, from previous organizations they have worked at. As a result, you have an end user population that may have certain "preconceived notions". Developers may think SharePoint is nothing particularly special and end users may have pigeon-holed the whole platform into a type of advanced network shared drive (the famous "s-drive"). Yet, much of what your team and your end users "know" is actually incomplete. For instance, SharePoint obviously offers far more capability than document management, but your end users may have put SharePoint into this pigeon hole. In some cases what your team "knows" is actually outright inaccurate.

Anti-patterns

Let's discuss an anti-pattern in some detail to illustrate all the previous discussions. An organization in the southern United States adopted SharePoint and rolled it out to their end user community. Like many organizations, the rollout was very shallow in nature and end users used SharePoint primarily for light document management. IT management, knowing that the platform was underutilized cast about for a business case to build a solution on SharePoint so that they could derive greater value from their SharePoint investment and ultimately settled upon a ticket management solution owned by the marketing and sales department. The goal was to automate how sales reps could order tickets on behalf of their customers and prospects from a pool of available tickets to local sports events (basketball, American football, and hockey).

They went through an appropriately rigorous requirements gathering and definition process for this surprisingly complex business process. IT's first mistake was to commit to delivering this solution on SharePoint with a deeply experienced .NET team who lacked experience with SharePoint (except as end users themselves). To top it off, they committed to an unrealistic delivery date. Of course, the delivery date didn't feel unrealistic at that time because the IT Team had delivered similar projects before — just not in SharePoint.

To cut a long story short, the team did deliver a solution on SharePoint and in the promised timeline. However, they crafted a solution characterized by the following anti-patterns:

- They developed the entire user interface as standalone ASP.NET web parts that were integrated with SharePoint via Page Viewer web parts (which is shorthand for saying they were not really integrated with SharePoint at all).

- They leveraged SharePoint security for the mere purpose of identifying whether a user was part of a group (that is, a simple lookup). No other part of SharePoint security was used. They had to roll their own security model within this supposed SharePoint application.

- They did not follow the SharePoint solution framework and instead relied upon an XCOPY deployment strategy. They didn't realize this was an issue until they added a new web frontend to the farm and everything broke.

- They created a side database to store lookup tables and transactional information that could have been and probably should have been stored in SharePoint custom lists and document libraries.

- They created an elaborate set of `web.config` modifications that required production system downtime for even minor changes to the application.

In the end, they had created a "SharePoint" application that used a bare fraction of the SharePoint functionality. As if the list of issues they've had isn't enough, their upgrade to SharePoint 2010 was greatly complicated by these poor technical decisions. Luckily, they took the time to refactor the application to work in SharePoint 2010, and in the long run these problems were solved. As with the insurance company example discussed earlier, the decisions were reasonable and appropriate from a traditional .NET point of view. However, they were actually insufficient when it came to working with SharePoint specifically.

Q: How do we decide upon our first project's scope?

A: Should you expect the solution to be a pilot or something that goes into production and stays in production for a year or longer? This is a key question that should be asked.

Project scope is an early key indicator that predicts the success of your first project. Consider the risks of an overly narrow project scope. Even if you succeeded in hitting project milestones and blow end user expectations off the roof, what have you really accomplished? It may be an important political victory, but this book isn't about political victories. You could be setting a bad precedent for future projects by having set unrealistically high expectations. This has happened before when a project team configured a SharePoint document library with a few content types and list views. It met the needs of the target business user group brilliantly. However, the project team didn't gain any great new understanding about SharePoint. When they took on their next project that involved using event receivers to populate intelligent default values on a list and communicate to an external web service, which ironically was of less business value than the pilot, the project team struggled and made a wreck of the schedule timeline. It wasn't a fatal blow, but it did create a negative experience and understanding of SharePoint.

Of course, you must avoid the opposite too. Don't select a major project with far-reaching implications for the business. You may never succeed in the first place.

When you think about scope, you need to think in both business and technical terms.

Principles of good business scope

To begin, business scope for a SharePoint project is no different from business scope for any other project. Ultimately business value must be in the solution. The same principles apply here as they do to any other business solution you would have your team implement. However, the business scope discussion is somewhat different with SharePoint and is more about strategy than putting a box around the solution. Your first SharePoint project's scope should follow these three principles:

- **Target a small number of users for the initial project**: This will tend to limit the technical implementation, which is your greatest source of risk in your first project. It also allows you to foster a great working relationship with the team, which leads to the next principle.

- **Select flexible business units**: The first project will be rocky. Your team may give mixed signals to the end users as they could be brimming with confidence (recall that SharePoint is "just a .NET application"). Beyond all of the usual miscommunications and not-quite-on-the-same-page moments any project suffers, you also need to deal with a new technology. If your end user business units aren't flexible, they may not prove to be supportive, as described in the next principle.

- **Do everything you can to ensure that your end user business unit is a good champion on your behalf**: So ideally this business unit should have a good working relationship with IT and yourself.

By defining an appropriately sized business scope, you've significantly reduced the risk you take on with your first SharePoint project. You can further reduce the risks by narrowing the technical scope.

Technical scope

The ideal technical scope is somewhere between too simple and too complex. That's easy to say, but how do you know in advance that you're going down the middle path? Let's consider the four most common types of SharePoint customizations that require programming:

- **Event receivers**: These programs run when end users upload new documents, change document metadata, or delete documents. They do the same for list items (for example, SharePoint calendar lists) except that they execute when the user creates, updates, or deletes a list item.

- **Timer jobs**: Similar to Unix cron jobs, Windows Services, and Windows scheduled tasks, a SharePoint timer job executes code on a periodic basis. The SharePoint platform installs dozens of timer jobs and you can create your own.

- **Custom web parts**: These are small programs that follow a handful of development rules. Web parts do not run on their own, but rather in the context of a SharePoint web page (in fact, web parts are a broader .NET artifact, but this discussion is confined to SharePoint for obvious reasons). As with timer jobs, SharePoint installs dozens of web parts. You can also create your own.

- **Visual Studio workflow**: SharePoint is based upon Microsoft .NET framework version 3.5, which includes a workflow engine, and you can leverage this engine in SharePoint.

Beyond coding, SharePoint offers several other customization options that lie somewhere in between coding and what your typical power user would do:

- Workflows using SharePoint Designer: Microsoft provides a friendly end user interface to .NET's workflow engine by way of a wizard-style GUI. "Friendly" is in the eye of the beholder and it's not unusual, especially in a SharePoint 2010 world, for developers to create workflow solutions using SharePoint Designer workflow capabilities.

- SharePoint Designer for customizing the UI.

- InfoPath for custom forms, often linked to workflow processes.

Lastly, companies take advantage of a very common use case, **jQuery**. jQuery is a JavaScript library that simplifies using JavaScript in a wide array of web development contexts, including SharePoint.

Bottom line: focus on one web part, one event receiver, or one event receiver and one timer job. Visual studio Workflow Foundation (WF) may not be a good first choice, especially a state machine WF (developers are always wanting to create state machine WFs).

Sirens of Greek mythology

As we wrap up this section, it's important to point out a peculiar problem that SharePoint may create. Similar to the Sirens whose songs lured Greek sailors to their deaths, SharePoint has its own peculiar song that seems to drive SharePoint developers, business analysts, and even ordinarily sober book authors to over-engineer solutions for their end users. Let's consider a real-world example.

A client described a set of requirements for a Legal and Medical Review (LMR) process. The SharePoint developer and his team worked with the end users using traditional requirements gathering techniques and then designed a solution to meet the requirements using SharePoint. The design was beautiful. It automated every action down to the last click of the mouse. It had branding, complex workflows, personalized e-mail notifications, and practically made coffee for you. It was a souped-up Cadillac with a gold plate and everything else you could think of. The effort it took to deliver the solution came to about 1,800 billable hours. The client balked at the hefty price tag and asked, "Why is this one business process going to cost me more to develop than it cost me to buy SharePoint in the first place?" It was a sobering moment and the team went back to the drawing board, producing an acceptable design that was 80 percent less effort to implement. This reduced effort design didn't meet 100 percent of the end users' requirements, but it met close to 90 percent of them and was far simpler than the original design. With the revised design, the tool could be built faster with less risk, be maintained easier and with less cost, and upgraded to the newest version of SharePoint with much less hassle than the original design. The moral of the story is that just because SharePoint can be extended in myriad ways using a host of technical means does not mean that it should be. This is true, of course, for any other kind of application in the world. However, SharePoint seems to suck architects and developers into an over-engineering mindset. Be aware of the pull and resist it.

Technical skill set

There is often focus on end user training but technical training is also the key, particularly for .NET developers. For example, many experienced techies are shocked to learn that there is no use case for direct database reads, let alone updates, to the SharePoint SQL database backend; it is always brokered through the SharePoint API layer. Knowing this in advance will help you plan your first project carefully.

Q: How do you plan for and design your first SharePoint project solution?

A: Planning your first SharePoint project isn't much different from planning for any other project. The project manager on your team works with end users and developers to identify tasks, estimate the resources required, and establish a projected completion date.

The key differences are the question to ask. Are we using the OOB functionality such as SharePoint Designer and the web power user configuration process, or does this require .NET development? Another question that should be asked is, does our deployed SharePoint edition have enough for the requirements? Maybe SharePoint Enterprise is required.

To view editions you can visit the following site:

```
http://sharepoint.microsoft.com/en-us/buy/Pages/Editions-Comparison.
aspx
```

These are infrastructure questions that need to be planned out to build an application.

Planning

There is one overall difference between this first SharePoint project and other web development projects your team has delivered in the past, the **Software Development Life Cycle (SDLC)** process. It's a real doozy the first time around and you'll want your team to learn these important bedrock technical concepts sooner rather than later.

The SDLC process for SharePoint isn't hard to understand and fundamentally follows good practices. Individual developers/consultants do their work on their development machine, then they deploy their solution to an integration server (where all of the different developers' work is merged) and then to a QA/Test environment where end users test the solution. Eventually, that approved solution is moved to production. The good news is that SharePoint provides excellent support for this process; however, the devil is in the details with testing in a production environment.

If this was a development project SharePoint defines and provides a "solution and feature framework". This framework defines the notion of a "solution", which is similar to a `.zip` file. Developers create these WSP files and deploy them to a SharePoint environment via a command-line tool. WSP files themselves include multiple different components called **features**. A feature is a cohesive unit of business functionality that could include some or all of the following SharePoint deployment components:

- Web parts
- Content type definitions
- List definitions
- Workflows
- Event receivers

It takes some time to learn how to craft the various XML files that correctly define SharePoint features and the first time around, it can be daunting. This is especially true when it comes to updating an existing solution. However, it's a skill well worth learning and should be integrated with your project schedule.

By understanding the value of SharePoint's deployment capabilities the projects delivery process can be accelerated exponentially. But this knowledge is not normally in the realms of a straight .NET developer with no SharePoint experience.

So a question in the questions stage should include:

- What technologies are we planning to use?
- Do we have the skill set to fully leverage SharePoint's functionality and deployment approach?

Designing

One of the things that distinguish SharePoint from other technology development is SharePoint's unique ability to prototype solutions for end users. You should take advantage of this capability early and often.

This is huge because of the school of thought where the business analyst documents the requirements, then the users sign off process or technology with which they are not familiar. The authors have experienced this sometimes when a company first installs SharePoint and starts an over-ambitious project and insists the business signs off on the requirements in the planning phase, only for the users to express that they really want something different.

IT leadership usually hears the business users' complaints and reacts by trying to "nail down" the requirements even harder by more rigorous and complicated methodologies changes. More meetings, more documents, and especially signoff contracts to force the user to agree on what will be done are an attempt to deflect any finger pointing later on. The result is normally a low-value solution and a poorly viewed first SharePoint project.

SharePoint-based prototyping only goes so far, of course. You may want to create some functionality that doesn't have a good analog in SharePoint today. In these cases, use prototyping tools. **Balsamiq** is one such tool and is very popular in the SharePoint community.

 Balsamiq allows you to rapidly create a sketch view on your computer screen with a simple drag-and-drop interface. Balsamiq is by no means unique; you could use Mockflow or Axure to name just a few.

For further information:

- **Balsamiq**: http://www.balsamiq.com/
- **Mockflow**: http://www.mockflow.com/
- **Axure**: http://www.axure.com/

These are low/medium/expensive options in that order.

These prototyping tools in the hands of a SharePoint **Subject Matter Expert (SME)** substantially improve the quality of your user requirements gathering process and reduce the risk of setting incorrect expectations with your end user partners. The next section, *What's the best way to execute?* dives more deeply into this last point.

The following screenshot illustrates the Balsamiq user interface and how a screen can be drafted to provide a user page layout:

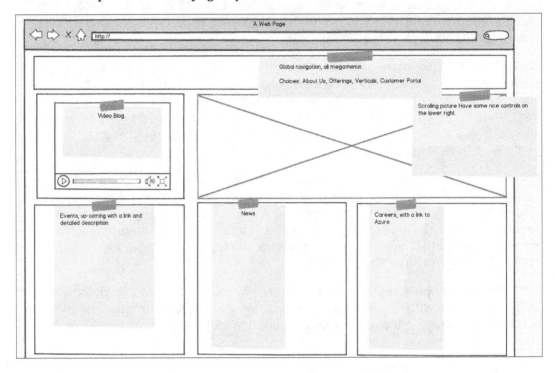

Q: What's the best way to execute?

A: Executing and implementing a SharePoint project can and should be a very exciting and rich experience for your end user business units.

Work iteratively

This is due to the fact that you can show intermediate work frequently throughout the process. You should build many checkpoints into your first project schedule where you demonstrate the current state of the solution to your end users and engage them in the process. You'll get a number of great benefits from this "show and tell" cycle:

- **Keeping on track**: If your team made a mistake, your end users will catch it for you right away and you can make the necessary adjustments and/or corrections immediately.

- **Making opportunistic changes to scope**: As you work through the solution side-by-side with the end users, both you and your partners will identify small configuration changes that could make a huge difference. You can take advantage of these SharePoint platform features (for example, adding a new list view) and deliver a higher-quality solution.

- **Create some buzz**: As end users see the solution get ever closer to its final deliverable state, they will become more excited and ready for that go-live moment. They will also likely talk it up with their peers in other business units, which answers a question asked later in this chapter. We'll cover that in a moment.

End users are not the only ones that benefit from these kinds of interim deliverables, which could be part of the XP or Agile deployment process. Your development team should do the same, as described next.

Share, share, share

Most developers naturally want to share information and experiences with each other. Simply Google "SharePoint blog" and you'll find literally hundreds, if not thousands of SharePoint developers sharing their tips, tricks, and sometimes their frustrations with SharePoint. For the first project, however, it's even more important, since so many parts of this process will be new to the team. The project manager should schedule specific checkpoints for developers' "show and tell" sessions. Encourage the team to implement a round-robin style schedule of intra-team presentations on every key area of the technical solution. This will ensure that the knowledge gained by team member "A" is at least seeded to team member "B". This ensures that you have a knowledgeable and engaged team for the second and later SharePoint projects.

Q: Should you implement in phases?

A: The answer to this question is "no". If you think you need to phase out your first project, there's a good chance that you have taken on more work than you should. Work on a project scope that can be done in about a maximum of 12 weeks with your team (more on team makeup in a minute). You should aim to develop, test, and go live in production within that timeframe, plus or minus a few weeks.

If you successfully confine yourself to a deliverable scope that fits within this timeframe, you can avoid scope sprawl, and then a traditional development process similar to waterfall is entirely appropriate. That is to say:

- Gather, document, and obtain end user signoff on requirements
- Implement the technical solution (but showing intermediate work to end users throughout this process)
- Apply formal user acceptance testing (UAT)
- Deploy to production

If for some reason, you can't confine the scope, avoid this kind of process if you can and instead follow an agile process, such as **SCRUM**. This is a topic outside the scope of this chapter and book. However, agile processes are entirely appropriate to follow with SharePoint projects. For more information, just google `SharePoint Agile Scrum` and you will find a great deal of useful information on this topic.

Funny you should say that...

This section explains some typical follow-up questions you may have once you start to think about your first SharePoint project.

Q: How do you organize your SharePoint team?

A: Your SharePoint project team won't break any of your old familiar patterns. The typical team consists of the following roles:

- **Project manager**: Manages the team to the schedule.
- **Business analyst**: Works closely with end users to obtain business requirements. Works with the technical team during implementation to answer business questions and provide quality control as the business solution is built.
- **SharePoint architect**: Ensures that the solution follows best practices for SharePoint. This includes infrastructure and security, coding and efficiency.
- **SharePoint developer(s)**: Implement the solution in code.
- **Quality assurance**: Test the solution.

In many cases, the first project's scope is small enough that you would have a team like this:

- One part-time Project Manager.

- One part-time Business Analyst. Sometimes, the PM serves both as PM and analyst.

- One full-time SharePoint Architect. The architect often does some coding.

- One or two SharePoint Developers.

- One QA person. Sometimes, the QA role is filled by the BA person, the PM person, or any combination of the three.

Or if this is really a small project then this may sufficient:

- Business Analyst/Project Manager, and Frontend Developer also known as a SharePoint Solution Architect.

The most appropriate team members may not be your "best" .NET coders, particularly if there is not custom development work. As we discussed in the planning phase, one of the key goals of a project is to build up the team's knowledge base. Your best architect and developer may not be the ideal candidate for sharing knowledge. You know your team, so be sure to staff the project with a knowledge sharing environment in mind and balance that need against the need for technical skills.

Q: How do you leverage success?

A: This simple question begs another question, "Why do I need to leverage success?" or more to the point "How is leveraging success with this first SharePoint project any different from leveraging success in other projects?". If you want SharePoint to be truly transformational rather than merely a collection of one-off business solutions, you need to find a way to parley your first project's success into something bigger. After all, if you follow the advice this chapter offers, your first project hasn't exactly boiled the ocean. That's not to say that it's low value, but you've deliberately crafted a solution that is relatively narrow in scope in order to reduce the significant risks that the first SharePoint project entails.

The solution is a joint road show with your end user business partner. After your customer has gone live with the solution and is living with the benefits of the project, create a presentation that touches upon the following points:

- What did you do? Emphasize the business problem and the solution.

- What benefit did the company realize from this effort?

- How long did it take and what did it cost? Don't forget to include costs to your end user partner, especially in terms of hours spent.

- Most importantly, how does this real-life in-production solution represent unexploited potential elsewhere in the company?

The objective of the road show is to motivate other business units to step up to the plate and request their own business solutions. You'll know you've been successful when the queue is 10 city blocks long. Of course, that presents a new set of challenges but that's a topic for a different book altogether.

You can reduce these risks and use this first project as a launching pad to SharePoint transformational nirvana by working closely with end users in a highly iterative manner. Show them intermediate work product to stay on track and make opportunistic enhancements to the solution in midstream. Build these intermediate reviews into your project schedule as well as intra-team technical "show and tells" designed to build up your internal SharePoint expertise and comfort levels.

When you finish, close it out with a joint road show with your end user business partner. Nothing sells like success in having a joint presentation with your satisfied customer and happy end users.

Digging deeper

Now you are probably thinking where your first SharePoint project can be deployed. This section has some questions that you should be asking.

Q: What problems should you anticipate with your first project?

A: There's a learning curve in understanding the SharePoint Framework, knowing how to deploy solutions, and managing users' expectations.

Q: Who should be the first business unit for a SharePoint deployment?

A: This depends and this question is addressed in *Chapter 1, Defining a SharePoint IT Strategy*.

A good tip is to avoid the sales department or any business unit that is very busy and does not have the time to provide requirements, or be trained. Sales folks can be classified into this group. They are rarely in the office, often resistant to technology change if it requires an investment of their immediate time, and when they are vocal that sales targets are being jeopardized because of time spent on a SharePoint project, continued management support can be unlikely.

This could be the same in any department.

Another challenge that you should consider is working with a user base that works in the building so water-cooler talk is possible. Yes, this informed dialogue to understand what is going on is huge.

Q. How easy is it to change from configuration to customization in a project?

A: If you have started a project with OOB features of SharePoint, communicate to the business unit that this is the approach at the start of the project, so expectations are leveled. Explain the pros and cons of this approach:

- **Pros**: Costs less to develop because we are leveraging the SharePoint technology, quicker delivery of the solution
- **Cons**: We are working with a template (SharePoint) and there are going to be limits

If requirements do change, particularly during the last 10 percent of the project, try to make these requirements a phase-two activity, so the project is not delayed and the value of the technology is deployed to the business.

Summary

Your first SharePoint project is a risky endeavor and this chapter has explained some considerations that are important to increase the likelihood that the project will be successful. You can see that you will need to manage a wide array of expectations and preconceived notions from both your end user business partners and your development team, with a defined right amount of scope for the project—too little and you may win the battle but lose the expectations; too much and you may lose the battle and have to regroup entirely.

Chapter 6, How to get the .NET Developers on Board Quickly? is very relevant to this chapter if .NET development is a requirement.

The following chapter is the final chapter of the book and wraps up all the chapters of the book into actionable steps for any business manager.

9
Now What?

This chapter demystifies the SharePoint product from a business manager's perspective in creating a starting point of where to begin planning and deploying the SharePoint technology within your organization.

With the knowledge obtained from the book such as deployment approaches, IT strategies, scaling, and .NET development, this chapter's intent is to provide "sticking power" to this knowledge.

Q: How do I apply the concepts from this book to produce results?

A: Great question. Remember, *knowing* makes no difference. Everyone *knows* the benefits of SharePoint technology, but that doesn't mean you will have increased efficiency by just *knowing*. So how do you deliver the business results? Only *actions* will produce any results with SharePoint.

The chapters intentionally cover most topics and questions that management or other decision-makers ask when they know they have to manage a SharePoint project. Each chapter is built on understanding and mastering the knowledge and concepts of the previous chapter. By the time you have reached this chapter, you either have all the answers, or know all the questions to ask to move forward and not be stopped in taking actions.

We recommend the best approach for action to occur is to:

- Discuss the concepts covered in this book with other members of your technical team
- Brainstorm, share, and create a vision and a game plan

- Create action plans with dates to fulfill and deliver goals

 Remember that what gets seen, gets measured. So when the action plan is agreed upon, share it with other departments, and other relevant management. Make sure everyone is on the same page, working towards the common vision and goals.

Q: I have heard SharePoint projects often fail. How can this be avoided?

A: There is usually not one single cause or agreement on why a project failed.

From our experience and observations, it's likely that the project did not have "company buy-in", was too complicated, project deliveries, if present at all, were not defined clearly enough, and/or other projects had a greater priority.

It doesn't have to be this way. Here are some observations that keep a SharePoint implementation project on track:

- SharePoint deployment is not about technology, but about business's processes. The first step in any SharePoint implementation must be to find out how things are really being done in a department and not what the training manual describes as the process. This is discussed in *Chapter 8, Managing your First SharePoint Project.*

- SharePoint adoption requires that users alter the way they have always done things. This means leaving their comfort zone and people don't like change. They tend to resist, complain, and often go back to the current process. Unless the users are involved from the beginning, a new SharePoint solution is something done to them and they feel powerless. The people doing the work are invaluable assets in the task of trying to make their job more efficient. Make sure you define SharePoint Governance, engage your users from both business and technical perspectives, looking critically at user requirements from both camps. This is discussed in *Chapter 2, Just Enough Governance.*

- Wisely choose and train a cross-organizational team with set goals and priorities. The best and the brightest users from each department make good working partners with senior management when designing new systems. That way, no one gets surprised by the costs in terms of money or effort when implementation time comes around. Creating a cooperative atmosphere, of course, is key to making this work. This is discussed in *Chapter 7, Growing SharePoint Capacity and Meeting Staffing Resource Needs.*

- Identify system requirements without alienating the users or future projects for the SharePoint technology. This is discussed in *Chapter 3, Deployment Roadmap*.

Prepare the users to adapt to the changes required by the new system. This was discussed in *Chapter 1, Defining a SharePoint IT Strategy*, with the deployment roadmap that outlined training and support to the user base.

Q: How do I choose a company to partner with?

A: After you have defined your SharePoint strategy (covered in *Chapter 1, Defining a SharePoint IT Strategy*) you may have decided to work with a Microsoft partner to deploy the SharePoint technology for an initial project. This is something that we recommend, because there is a certain predictability that the installed outcome will be correct on the first installation.

The *fake it till you make it* (after many attempts you will get it right) approach on an installation is expensive both in time and productivity and ultimately hard earned trust from the business users who may question why there are technical issues causing delays with a project.

We recommend the following steps in choosing a business and technical partner:

- **Check out their website**: If their website is built with SharePoint, the probability is that they have in-house SharePoint expertise. They are practicing what they preach, so to speak. If their website is really slick, you could ask them how the site is built.

- **Identify their Microsoft partner status**: To obtain a certain status level with Microsoft, the business partner must have certain competencies, and passing certain technical exams. This ensures consultants are qualified and familiar with the SharePoint technology. Therefore, one of the keys in selecting a partner is to work with one that has a Gold partner status with an Information Worker competency. This means that they have a focus with the SharePoint technology.

Every couple of years Microsoft overhauls its partner qualification program. It currently offers certification in 28 competencies. The trend is that Gold status is more exclusive. For more information, take a look at `https://partner.microsoft.com/40011230`.

- **Ask for references**: You can always call Microsoft for a recommendation. Your Microsoft account manager works closely with partners in your area and can provide an introduction and/or recommendation. Speak with the references identified by your potential partner and ask for specific reactions and/or responses during the implementation stage, especially when things don't go as planned. With any project, there are bound to be bumps on the road. Get a sense if the potential business partner is accommodating, flexible, and responsive to your needs.

Beware that the Microsoft account manager will have his or her preferred partners and they may not always be the best fit for your requirements. So be sure to ask for the rationale and explanation behind the recommended partners as well as cultural fit.

- Write an Request For Proposal (RFP) and submit to the various partners in your area.

Q: Is it easy to offshore SharePoint development?

A: The ease of offshore SharePoint development depends on an organization's approach. Every offshore development project, regardless of the platform, faces similar issues such as time zone differences, language, and cultural barriers. There are three additional challenges that affect the off shoring of SharePoint development:

- **SharePoint Development requires close interaction with end users**: Having a clear plan and the appropriate team members is key to making offshore SharePoint development successful. They must be treated as an augmentation to your existing team. It is not enough to have a business analyst in-house or on-site to collect requirements and pass them off to the offshore development team to code. A senior SharePoint architect is necessary to make architectural decisions and to lead quality assurance, testing, deployment, and adoption. An offshore team simply will not have the access to end users that is required for effective and responsive development.

- **Best development practices and standard processes are not entirely defined or finalized for SharePoint**: ASP.NET development is a much more mature practice and it still has changing standards. Organizations should not depend on an offshore team to deliver code that supposedly adheres to best practices and processes. For this reason it is important to have SharePoint resources on-site or in-house to manage quality, best practices, and risk.

- **SharePoint developers require constant access to server environments**: Server environment access is necessary for testing, configuration, and deployment. Server stability is crucial and becomes vulnerable and prone to compromise when the average developer has access that allows him or her to make changes on the server. An in-house development team or a senior SharePoint resource can help overcome this challenge.

A senior SharePoint resource is in-house to help bridge the gaps that an offshore team creates. Offshore SharePoint development can be very effective as team augmentation, however, we do not recommend off shore resources for the main development and delivery team to the business.

An author worked on a project where the SharePoint development was off-shored to a third-party company and they were not allowed access to the company's development environment. So all releases were zipped up and e-mailed to the in-house developer to install in the company environment. With the end user interaction and feedback, any cost saving of the offshore approach was negated with the endless redeploying of code. What should have occurred is that the off-shoring company has access to the company development environment, so they deploy the code each time and the user base does not need to wait until lunch time for the new release to be ready.

Q: How do I estimate a SharePoint development project?

A: Like most projects, most developers tend to be optimistic with their estimates of time and resources. There are no simple answers or rules that one can follow to assure accurate estimates, but an experienced developer might consider the following to help drive more accurate assessments and estimates:

- Vague and changing requirements lead to inaccurate estimates. Although this is a general rule for all development projects, SharePoint can introduce unique complexities. At times the simplest shift in requirement can cause great discrepancies in estimates. Remember, developers are working with an already established product and "small" customizations can turn out to be a "large impact" customization in SharePoint.

- There are several approaches to help solidify vague requirements. A Gap Analysis is where one highlights how SharePoint, out of the box functionality, fulfills some or all requirements and where custom development will be needed to help flush out requirements. This way, each requirement that is addressed by out of the box functionality can be solidified up front by the existing functionality of SharePoint. Requirements that need custom development can be explored further and solidified.

- Take time to evaluate and prepare a development environment. The goal with development environments is for them to resemble production environments as much as possible. Any security setting, account access, server configuration, or discrepancy in SharePoint or software license can cause major drawbacks in the later stages of development (that is testing and deployment). Part of the estimate should include setup or verification of development environments.

- Part of any development project is not just estimating the actual development time but also estimating the testing and deployment time. Testing and deployment will occur in multiple environments (that is development, staging, and production environments). Just because a customization passed all tests in development does not mean it will pass in staging, let alone production. Make sure you estimate time to test throughout the environments and not just test customization. Regardless of how much you try to mirror environments, it is unattainable.

- An understanding for the technical environment and the access privileges that a developer has been granted is necessary. If code is off loaded to a Delivery Manager person, they may not be fully aware of how to deploy and test and time is wasted.

 There are few more frustrating experiences for a developer than to explain how to deploy their code to the live environment and troubleshoot it to another person who is not knowledgeable about the code and functionality. This is a major time drain on a project.

A complex production environment is simply not feasible to recreate in development or even in a staging environment. The complexity of environments introduces factors that were non-existent and impossible to simulate in development environments.

 With delays, expectations must be managed. Remember the business sponsor not concerned with release problems or the governance implementations. All they really want to know is when the project will go live and deliver business results.

Q: How easy is it for Java development teams to learn .NET SharePoint development?

A: In true Microsoft style, Microsoft technology normally works best with its development tools. In fact people in Redmond probably could not spell Java.

You probably can mix and match the .NET and JEE technologies together, but this is an unpredictable approach with limited support options.

Java developers can easily learn .NET SharePoint development. There are two matters that influence the ease of making the switch:

- Although you need to learn a new language and a new or unique syntax (Java to C# or VB .NET), the good news is that Java and these languages are very similar. This makes the learning curve less steep. Both sets of languages are object oriented, so they share the same basic development principles.
- A Java developer will need to be familiar with ASP.NET development. Issues that are unique to ASP.NET and not necessarily Java developers are, managing page lifecycle, hosting and security, and different development tools. Scenarios, issues, and problems may be different, but the building blocks remain the same; the way you structure and build code is the same in Java and .NET.

In the end, Java developers can easily apply their understanding of code and how it acts to learning .NET development. In turn, knowledge and understanding of .NET development will enable the developer to quickly adopt SharePoint.

Funny you should say that...

This section explains some typical follow-up questions you may have once you start to think about how to apply information from this book.

Q: How do I write an RFP for a technology that I'm not familiar with?

A: A **Request for Proposal (RFP)** should be written with care and by someone with SharePoint knowledge. If that's not you, (which we suspect it's not since you're reading this book!) you may have to hire a SharePoint consultant for at least a few weeks to understand your business requirements and define the appropriate required SharePoint technology.

For the following reasons, we have our reservations about the RFP process, but it is a common practice in the IT industry, so do take care throughout.

You get what you ask for

Remember an RFP is essentially a one-way message you are communicating to your potential business partner about what is required of the SharePoint system within your organization. In some situations, the prospective partner will ask questions that require clarification on one or more of the RFP questions. In certain cases, the prospective partner may not answer a question. You should find out why. This may be a telltale sign about their willingness and/or competency, or reveal other reasons for concern. Thus the individuals answering your RFP are left to assume a great deal while responding and this is when these assumptions bite back. You got it—user acceptance of the delivery, the very people who will make or break the success of your SharePoint solution.

> Do not assume the implementation partner is on the hook to deliver assumptions that are out of scope.

The challenges of the delivery of this first SharePoint project are discussed in *Chapter 8, Managing your First SharePoint Project*.

People are fooled by price

Price should not be the single deciding factor in accepting an RFP. One of the key assumptions that you must make is the price of the system. Because the dialog between buyer and seller is limited, prices for software and services are almost always erroneous. This favors the disingenuous vendor who can purposely lower the estimate and point to faulty assumptions later. If the buyer's prescription is a fixed-fee implementation, then ask for specific plans and estimated time frame and make sure to also build in additional time to the project, just in case an assumption is in the vendor's favor.

While you may be lured by the initial lower prices, often, due to faulty assumptions or delayed/added scope, the cost of the project will exceed your initial budget and timeline, which results in an unhappy in-house technical support team, unhappy end users, and ultimately unhappy upper management. The response to the RFP contains a list of features and functionality with the intent of distinguishing which software application has the best features.

Let's face it now. If you are sending your RFP to prime-time players, they will pretty much have all the core required functionality you are seeking. The fact is that an RFP will not weed out vendors based on functionality because the vendor is unable to show their work to existing clients. Make sure you take the time to obtain the right information from the business, and end users and apply this to the RFP. Also see examples of the vendors work and perhaps a presentation from their team.

 It's more expensive to pick a wrong vendor because you didn't spend enough time defining your business goals, scope, and constraints.

Time is money

Which brings us to the point that a tremendous amount of time is wasted by both buyer and seller as a result of the RFP ritual. First, think about the time spent on creating the RFP itself; the days and sometimes weeks it takes for each firm to answer the RFP, and then there is the process of evaluating the RFP results. There is nothing scientific in saying that this amounts to hundreds of hours that could be devoted to making a decision in a more enlightened fashion. The RFP continues to be a time burglar after the purchase is made. Throughout the implementation process, as issues arise that were not foreseen during the sales process, the client will invariably refer to the RFP and the signed contract. We have seen implementations delayed by months while client and vendor dispute whether or not the answers to the RFP implied that the project should include certain large areas of functionality. This is valuable time that costs both parties a fair bit of money. If your company has corporate lawyers they may not be able to assist, because the assumptions are technical.

Beauty is in the eye of the beholder

We think the chief sin of the RFP process is that it forces vendors to compete over requirements that are created by prospects who assume they know what they need, and if you have never used SharePoint before this is impossible.

The fact is that each software developer possesses a unique vision of how they zcan solve business problems, not just through a checklist of features, but through an innovative approach utilizing continuously evolving technologies. The RFP process takes no account of the special value that each product possesses, and instead relying upon a dry list of features, which all the products in question would likely possess. In order to discover the unique proposition of any application, a prospective buyer should do everything possible to create an interactive dialog with the individual developers.

> If your organization insists that you must submit an RFP for a SharePoint project, a good approach is to ask vendors for examples of RFP that they responded to. Some vendors would be willing to do this to establish a relationship with you.

Digging deeper

Given this is the last chapter, you should be thinking about how to deploy SharePoint and what actions are required for this to occur. This section provides some further guidance to your thoughts.

Q: Can a SharePoint deployment really help my career?

A: Of course… No one ever got fired for buying Microsoft. Yeah right.

If SharePoint is deployed correctly, yes it can; but this is like any IT deployment. If SharePoint is new to your organization, there will probably be several people making requests for its functionality.

Deploying a SharePoint strategy to an organization can be a stop-go process, partly because SharePoint creates new processes, so there can be challenges in deliveries and user acceptance; but it does not need to be this way. During this process there are what are known as **Operating States** that groups, teams, and organizations go through in getting any project or task accomplished and changes required in their behavior.

If you are tasked with your organization's first SharePoint deployment and you observe and perform in these operating states then although there is no guarantee, there is a good chance that this deployment will be beneficial to your career, because the SharePoint initiative will likely succeed.

A description of the characteristics of each operating state is given next, and these are characteristics that are designed to empower you to be effective in fulfilling a project or a task in that operating state. They are not descriptions or facts. They are declarations that you make as a way to apply yourself effectively toward the fulfillment or accomplishment of a project.

Formulation

Formulation starts with creating and articulating an intention, such as defining a SharePoint strategy and announcing this to a department or management. You then staff this intention and design a project, including a clear statement of the outcomes or results you intend to produce. In formulating a project you specifically determine what you and others are accountable for. You set up structures for communication and design the ground rules for working (that is, who reports to whom).

Once this is complete, you announce your intention and project and you make yourself known to this organization, as well as the fact that this is your project. Finally, you determine what the current reality for the project is, such as skills required and available technology.

Recognize that there may be almost nothing in existence to support your intention initially. As this is a new initiative to the organization, people may require training and new organizational structures may need to be outlined.

Concentration

Concentration is about focusing on the project and determining what is required to get things moving, what actions there are to take, what there is to do, and so on. You then promise to do something, and do it! At this stage you begin to bring SharePoint functionality to the user and business. This takes a very concentrated effort. This state tends to require very high activity on your part with very little return initially. You have to demonstrate to yourself and others that you can produce the result you said you would produce when you said you'd produce it.

Working in a concentration state requires discipline and focus, so it may mean working at home, or a Saturday morning. What is key is that you think about what actions are required and what you are trying to do with this project. It is best done without interruption. This is where you planned your work and worked your plan

Momentum

After working in a Concentration state and having started to produce some results over time, a project begins to gain some **Momentum** and user acceptance is occurring with SharePoint initiatives. You start to gain power and effectiveness with other managers and technical staff. Results start to equal the actions and activities you are putting into this project. In a Momentum stage, you want to start to promote what you are accomplishing and make it well thought of. You want to swing out a little and risk yourself. Start making big promises. Inspiration and spontaneity start to occur. You want to start enrolling others in participating with the SharePoint technology and you start providing guidance and be seen as a business partner versus a forced technology deployment.

You must always watch yourself and others at this stage because any momentum will come to a halt if you stop working and start thinking something will happen on its own.

Stability

Stability is about completing the small wins of a project in a reliable state, which requires that you demonstrate being able to work on similar processes and tasks repetitively and routinely. This state requires being very well organized and in many cases having things automated with typical SharePoint projects, such as requirement documents, functionality releases to the business, change requests, and help desk support. In this operating state you systemize, structure, and plan to implement the SharePoint technology to other business processes (see *Chapter 1, Defining a SharePoint IT Strategy,* for an approach). Start to measure more and create new statistics to monitor. There will soon be a surplus of results and you can start managing the project from the point of view of empowering others to produce the results with this technology.

[Don't change anything that is working and don't experiment without having reliable structures in place.]

Breakthrough

In the **Breakthrough** operating state there is a sudden, unexpected rise in the results, such as a large project request by the CEO of the company. Things speed up and you must demonstrate that you can handle power and velocity. In this operating state you work on your ability to deliver. You manage the project in this operating state with complete and powerful communication with your team and stakeholders. Make sure that everyone involved in the project is supported and organized. Any breakdowns that happen should immediately become an opportunity to produce a new result and should be dealt with in that way.

Do not get fascinated with the results.

Mastery

This operating state is concerned with key projects being fulfilled. Not only will the results have been produced but also the project will be completed and/or turned over to others to manage. In this operating state there isn't anything that's incomplete. It is about the domain of excellence. In this operating state the original intention is fulfilled but the project tends to have a life of its own and continues to be operational. You, the originator of the intention and the project tend to focus on other larger strategic SharePoint projects because the intention and the project now belong entirely to others.

If you feel that you have reached the **Mastery** operating state, then your peers will recognize this and acknowledge you for your effort and your ability to repeat this success.

These operating states could be identified as a standard project management methodology that could be applied to any result-based activity. This is not unique to a SharePoint project, but they are very effective with SharePoint activities, which tend to linger on for far too long and never get completed, such as Governance policies or a training strategy. The effectiveness of the defined operating states is because each state identifies the kind of human behavior that is required to achieve results with new activities and projects that an individual is unfamiliar with.

We have seen readers apply these operating states to business-related activities and achieve their goals.

By applying the operating states to SharePoint initiatives that you are working on, the success rate is definitely in your favor, which means your SharePoint projects are being deployed and hopefully recognized across the organization. This is how the SharePoint technology can help your career.

Other operating states

Emergency and **Danger** are operating states that come into play when a project slips from a higher operating state to a lower one.

Emergency

An **Emergency** occurs when there is action stopped and things become unworkable. This can occur when resources are shifted to another project or project dependencies are not ready in the agreed timelines. This can also happen because there is not enough action being taken or someone's actions have been ineffective. In an emergency, the project has slipped back one operating state.

It is not difficult to recognize when you are in this state. The key is to recognize how to get out of this state or prevent it. If possible, prevention is the best way.

Danger

A **Danger** state is a serious condition that requires immediate action. The project will have slipped back two operating states at this point and is on its way out of existence. This is almost always due to lack of actions from team members or in your own management. Work is not been getting done, based on the agreements of resources by when you said it would for some period of time. In this operating state you must acknowledge take responsibility with resources and project stakeholders, and clean up any issues of integrity and then apply Concentration.

Summary

This brings us to the end of the chapter and the book. In this chapter, you have been introduced to some concepts and ideas of how to apply the knowledge gained from this book with your first SharePoint project or initiative.

As ever, we hope that you will be as impressed as we are with Microsoft's SharePoint 2010 release and understand the challenges, pitfalls, and opportunities of deploying and managing the SharePoint technology. More than that, we hope that you have enjoyed not just this chapter, but also the book, and that it has helped you to understand SharePoint from a business management standpoint.

With any technology you wind up with one of two things — the results of a project or the reason why you don't have the results. Results don't have to be explained. They just are.

From all of the writers involved with this book, good luck!

Index

Symbols

.NET development
  about 31, 128, 141
  comparing, with SharePoint development
    128-132
  comparing, with SharePoint .NET 140
.NET Framework 128

A

Access 45, 47
Acing 103
Active Directory 23, 128, 137
Active Directory Directory Services (ADDS)
  83
Active Directory Federation Services. *See*
  ADFS 2.0
Active Directory Resources 155
ADFS 2.0 63, 89
agile 117
agile development methods 117-119
agile software development 117-119
AIIM 99, 101
Alltop
  URL 123
Amazon 81, 82
Amazon CloudWatch 80
Amazon Direct Connect 81
Amazon EBS 78, 79
Amazon EC2
  about 75, 78, 79
  capabilities 79
  URL 95

Amazon Elastic Block Store. *See* **Amazon
  EBS**
Amazon Elastic Compute Cloud. *See* **Amazon EC2**
**Amazon Identity Access Management
  (Amazon IAM) 91**
Amazon infrastructure 82
Amazon Machine Images (AMIs) 79, 81
Amazon Route 53 81
Amazon security
  about 91
  Amazon Identity Access Management
    (Amazon IAM) 91
  network ACLs 91
  security groups 91
Amazon Virtual Private Cloud. *See* **Amazon
  VPC**
Amazon VPC
  about 76-80
  URL 95
Amazon Web Services (AWS)
  about 76, 78
  Amazon EBS 78, 79
  Amazon EC2 78, 79
  Amazon VPC 78-80
  ELB 78, 80
  using, for SharePoint 2010 78
Anonymous 63
Apple iPad 100
authentication methods, SharePoint 2010 63
authentication options, SharePoint Online
  about 88
  ADFS 2.0 89
  Microsoft Online Services IDs 88

Microsoft Windows Live IDs 88, 89
SSO 89
authentication, SharePoint 2010
  about 63
  claim-based 63
  classic 63
Axure
  URL 181

B

Balsamiq
  about 181
  URL 181
Basic 63
basics areas, for governance 30, 31
benefits, ELB 80
benefits, Microsoft private cloud 85
benefits, on-premise deployment 48
BI, for masses 111, 112
Binary Large Objects (BLOBs) 61
BitLocker 92
BI tools, Microsoft 112, 113
BLOB storage 90
blogging 31
breakthrough operating state 200
Bristol-Meyers Squibb 63
budget 165
business analyst 184
Business Connectivity Services 44
Business Intelligence (BI) 111, 163
business unit, SharePoint deployment 186

C

capabilities, Amazon EC2 79
characteristics, Microsoft private cloud
  Microsoft Enrolment for Core Infrastructure
    licensing program 85
  technology Stack 84
chargeback strategy, SharePoint
  about 163
  charge per GB 163
  charge per site 163
  charge per user 163
CIO.com 123
Claims-Based Authentication 44, 64
Client Access License (CALs) 152

cloud computing
  about 51, 73
  Infrastructure as a Service (IaaS) 51
  Platform as a Service (Paas) 51
  Software as a Service (SaaS) 51
cloud deployment models, SharePoint 2010
  about 74
  community cloud 74, 77
  hybrid cloud 74, 77
  private-cloud 74, 76
  public cloud 74, 75
CMSWire
  about 101
  URL 123
CNN Technology 122
collaboration and communication trends
    101, 106-110
committee, SharePoint governance
  about 33, 34
  case study 34
communication skills, SharePoint developer
    146
community cloud 74, 77
complimentary SharePoint technology 138,
    139
concentration 199
Concurrent Version System (CVS) 132
consumer trends
  about 122
  resources 122
Content Database 151
content database storage
  estimating 60
content management 31
Content Migration 161
CRM 172
CRM system 36

D

danger operating state 201, 202
data and information trends 101, 110, 112
Data at Rest, SharePoint security
  about 92
  BitLocker 92
  Transparent Data Encryption (TDE) 92
Data in Transit, SharePoint security 91, 92

data scale 61
data storage 29
DELL 63
deployment strategy
  building 136
development 29
development environment
  about 133
  creating 134
development type, SharePoint
  backend .NET development 129
  frontend .NET development 129
device-based CAL (Device CAL) 53, 55
Digest 63
Disaster recovery (DR) farms 57
DocumentsToGo 66
Domain Name System (DNS) 128
Duet Enterprise 68

E

E1 plan 87
E2 plan 87
E3 plan 87
E4 plan 87
ECI Datacenter 85
ECM system 99
editions, SharePoint
  SharePoint Foundation 44
  SharePoint Server 2010 Enterprise 45
  SharePoint Server 2010 Standard 45
Elastic Load Balancing. See ELB
ELB
  about 78-80
  benefits 80
ELB, SharePoint architectural design
  Amazon CloudWatch 80
  Amazon Direct Connect 81
  Amazon Route 53 81
  Auto Scaling 80
emergency operating state 202
Engadget 122
Enterprise 2.0 108
Enterprise Content Management (ECM) 114
Enterprise Plans 87
Enterprise Site Collections Administrator
    155

environment security 117
ERP 172
essential skills, SharePoint developer 136,
    137
Eucalyptus 84
Excel 45, 47
existing licenses
  migrating 64, 65
extranet environment, SharePoint 62

F

farms 29
FAST
  and SharePoint 115, 116
FAST Search Server 2010
  for Internet Sites 47
  for SharePoint 2010 45, 46
features 180
Focus
  URL 123
Forbes Technology 122
Forefront Online 56, 86
For Internet Sites (FIS) 46
formulation 199
Forrester
  about 101
  URL 123
forums 149

G

GAP analysis 17, 20
Garbage In Garbage Out (GIGO) 111
Gartner
  about 101, 103, 107, 109
  URL 123
GigaOm
  URL 123
Git 133
Gizmodo 122
goals, for IT strategy 13, 14
Google 114
Google Alerts 123
governance
  about 30
  basics areas 30, 31
  need for 30

governance documentation
    activities 31
    issues, of hiring consulting firm 35
grow capacity 165

H

Harvard Business Review
    URL 123
**Health Insurance Portability and Account-
ability Act (HIPPA) 34**
HESS 63
hidden costs, SharePoint
    skill sets, for different company sizes 161,
    162
HIPAA 50
hosted deployment 49
HP Business Decision Appliance 68
HTML 132
Human Resources (HR) 166
hybrid cloud 74, 77
hybrid deployment 52
Hyper-V 84, 85 142

I

IDC
    about 101
    URL 123
Idera 93
IGT Cloud 77
industry and technology trends
    about 123
    resources 123
InfoPath 45, 47, 129, 132
InfoPath 2010 129
Information Architecture (IA) 99
Infrastructure as a Service (IaaS) 51, 73-75
in-house deployment. *See* **on-premise
deployment**
internal corporate trends 122
**Internet Information Services (IIS) 128, 137,
157, 172**
Intranet Benchmarking Forum
    URL 123
intranet environment, SharePoint 62
IT delivery trends 101-106

IT products
    versus SharePoint strategy 23, 24
IT steering committee
    about 33
    activities 33
IT steering committee, activities
    approval of IT projects 33
    IT project prioritization 33
    IT strategic planning 33
IT strategy
    about 12
    goals 13, 14
    need for 26, 27
IT trend information 99

J

Java development teams
    .NET SharePoint development, learning
    195
JavaScript 132
job description, SharePoint Developer 159
just enough governance 38

K

Kerberos 63
Key Performance Indicator (KPI) 112
key performance indicators (KPIs) 164
Kiosk Plan 86, 87
Kraft Foods 63

L

Legal and Medical Review (LMR) 178
Lego set 128
lemmatization 115
License Mobility
    through Microsoft Software Assurance 64
**Lightweight Directory Access Protocol
(LDAP) 63**
lists 128
Logical Units (LUNs) 61
Lync 108
Lync Communicator 107

M

Managed Metadata Service 45
Mashable 122
mastery operating state 201
Metalogix Migration Manager 93
MetaVis 93
Microsoft 100
Microsoft BI Stack 112
Microsoft Certified Architect (MCA) 118
Microsoft Certified Master (MCM) 118
Microsoft Developer Network. *See* MSDN
Microsoft Development Network. *See*
    MSDN
Microsoft Enterprise Agreement (EA) 56, 85
Microsoft Enterprise License Agreement
    164
Microsoft Office 365 47
Microsoft Office 365 for Education plan 87
Microsoft Office 2010
    integrating, with SharePoint 2010 67
Microsoft Office SharePoint Server 2007
    (MOSS 2007) 44
Microsoft Online Services 88
Microsoft Online Services Transition Center
    URL 96
Microsoft partner status
    identifying 191
Microsoft private cloud
    about 84
    benefits 85
    characteristics 84
    URL 95
Microsoft private cloud solution
    creating, for SharePoint 84
Microsoft products, for deployment
    antivirus 68
    Business intelligence 68
    client applications 69
    disaster recovery 67
    project management 68
    security 68
Microsoft SharePoint
    Duet Enterprise 68
Microsoft SharePoint Workspace 2010 69
Microsoft Windows Live IDs 88, 89
Microsoft Word 24

minimal SharePoint deployment 152, 153
Mobile Entrée 66
mobile phones 66
Mockflow
    URL 181
momentum 200
MSDN
    about 55, 57
    URL 127
MS Forefront Protection 2010 68
MS Forefront Threat Management Gateway
    2010 (TMG) 68
MS Forefront Unified Access Gateway 2010
    (UAG 68
MS products
    integrating, with SharePoint 2010 67
MS Project Server 68
MS System Center Data Protection Manager
    67
My Sites 23, 66, 67
MySites 31

N

network Access Control Lists (ACLs) 91
NTLM 63

O

Office 365
    about 75, 85, 95
    top-level offerings 86
Office 365 Dedicated 86
Office 365, for Enterprise Service Descrip-
    tions
    URL 95
Office 365 Plans
    URL 95
Office 365 Standard 86
offshore development project, SharePoint
    192, 193
on-premise deployment
    about 48
    benefits 48
    disadvantages 49
    mograting, to SharePoint Online 92-94

operating states, SharePoint deployment
  breakthrough 200
  concentration 199
  danger 202
  emergency 202
  formulation 199
  mastery 201
  momentum 200
  stability 200
Optum Health Cloud 77
organization
  IT trends 101
organization, trends
  about 101
  collaboration and communication 101,
    106-110
  data and information 101, 110, 112
  IT delivery 101, 105, 106
  user-experience 101-104
Outlook 107
out of the box (OOTB) 140, 119

P

pages 128
PerformancePoint 45, 47
Performance Point 2010 130
PerformancePoint Services 112
Phillip Morris International 63
PivotReader 103
Plan P 86
Platform as a Service (PaaS) 51, 73-75
PowerPivot 112
private cloud 74, 76, 95
production environment
  building 135
project management 31
project manager 184
public cloud 74, 75
Public Facing SharePoint Sites
  URL 70
public Internet presence, SharePoint
  about 63
  access 63
  functionality 63
  licensing 63

Q

QlikTech 111
quality assurance 184
quality assurance (QA) 57, 58
Quest Software 93

R

ReadWriteWeb
  URL 123
Real Story 101
recruiters 159
Remote BLOB Storage (RBS) 61
remote desktop protocol (RDP) 91
Request For Proposal (RFP) 192, 195-197
Return On Investment (ROI) 165
Risk Registry 22

S

SAML token-based 63
sandbox 134
Sandbox environment 156
SANS 59
SAP
  Duet Enterprise 68
Sarbanes-Oxley 50
SCRUM 184
SDLC process 180
search 113
Securities and Exchange Commission (SEC)
  34
Security Groups 91
security, SharePoint deployment
  Amazon security 91
  SharePoint security 91
security trends
  about 116
  environment security 117
  SharePoint permission sprawl 116, 117
server licenses 53
Server licensing model 54
Server plus CAL licensing model 54
SharePlus 66

SharePoint
  about 36, 37, 44, 100, 128
  agile development methods 118, 119
  and FAST 115, 116
  editions 44, 53, 54
  hidden costs 161, 162
  in-house technical staff, training 156
  listening, to recruiters on job descriptions 159
  Microsoft private cloud solution, creating for 84
  MS Forefront Protection 2010 68
  offshore development project 192, 193
  public Internet presence 63
  Return On Investment (ROI) 165, 166
  servers, running 55
  skill sets, for different company sizes 154, 155
  success, leveraging 185, 186
  team, organizing 184, 185
  technical skill 152, 153
  topologies, selecting 61
  training resources 156-158
  URLs, for authentication mechanisms 70
  URLs, for capacity planning 70
  URLs, for editions 69
  URLs, for extranet topologies 70
  using, for charge back model 162
  URL, for object model 128
SharePoint 2010
  Amazon Web Services (AWS), using 78
  authentication methods 63
  cloud deployment models 74
  development (DEV) 57, 58
  FAST Search Server 2010 45, 46
  integrating, with Office 2010 67
  licensing 53
  mobile phones 66
  MS products, integrating with 67
  production (PROD) 57, 58
  quality assurance (QA) 57, 58
  tablets 66
  web browsers 65
SharePoint 2010 deployment
  Amazon infrastructure layer 82
  authentication, for end users 63
  SharePoint infrastructure 84

  Windows infrastructure 83
SharePoint 2010 Foundation 151
SharePoint applications
  advantages, of buying over building 119
  rapid growth, reasons 120, 121
SharePoint architect 184
SharePoint Backup 161
SharePoint deployment
  about 47, 48
  business unit 186
  cloud 51
  help, in career 198
  hosted 49, 50
  hybrid 52
  on-premise 48
  requisites 59
  security 91
  strategy 59
SharePoint Designer 129, 132
SharePoint Designer 2010 69
SharePoint Designer 2010 (Free) 129
SharePoint developer
  about 184
  communication skills 146
  essential skills 136, 137
  job description 159
  mistakes 145
  mistakes, avoiding in early stages 139
  preferred requisites 160
SharePoint developer route
  resistance, reasons 143, 144
SharePoint development
  approaching 132
  books, for learning 150
  comparing, with .NET development 128-132
  connecting, through social media 148, 149
  customizations, deploying 141
  deployment strategy 136
  development environment, creating 133, 134
  features, functioning within platform 141
  forums 149
  learning 147
  production environment, building 135
  source control strategy 132, 133
  technical environment 142, 143

UAT environment, building 134, 135
user group, finding 148
SharePoint development project
estimating 193, 194
SharePoint Farm Administrator 154
SharePoint Foundation
about 44
deployment 151
SharePoint governance
balance 38
committee 33, 34
mission application 39
suggestions 40
URL, for further information 42
SharePoint Governance 29
SharePoint implementation plan 19, 20
SharePoint implementation project
observations, for keeping on track 190
SharePoint infrastructure 83
SharePoint IT strategy
CEO involvement 23
creating 15
people involvement 22
SharePoint IT strategy, workshop agenda
diagnostics 15, 17
outcomes 20, 21
SharePoint implementation plan 19, 20
treatment plan 17-19
SharePoint .NET
comparing, with .NET development 140
SharePoint Online
about 85
authentication options 88
limitations 94
missing features 94
on-premise deployment, migrating 92, 93, 94
SharePoint permission sprawl 116, 117
SharePoint Products and Technologies governance plan
URL, for sample template 32
SharePoint project
anti-patterns 174
business scope, principles 176
case study, for insurance organization 173
comparing, with technology project 172
configuration to customization 187

designing 179, 181
end user community 174
executing 182
factors, for considerations 170
implementing 182
implementing, in phases 183
issues 186
planning 179, 180
scope 176
Sirens, of Greek mythology 178
technical scope 177
technical skillset 179
SharePoint project, considerations
configuration versus customization 171
customers 171
scope 170, 171
size 170, 171
team skills and experience 170
SharePoint Saturdays 101
SharePoint security
Data at Rest 92
Data in Transit 91, 92
SharePoint Server 2010
for Internet Sites, Enterprise 47
for Internet Sites, Standard 46
SharePoint Server 2010 Enterprise 45
SharePoint Server 2010 Standard 45
SharePoint strategy
company, selecting for partnership 191, 192
pitfalls 25, 26
suggestions 27
versus IT products 23
SharePoint team
organizing 184, 185
SharePoint Workspace 103
SMART 17
Social Networking 2.0 31
Software as a Service (SaaS) 51, 73-75
Software Development Life Cycle. *See* SDLC process
Sony PlayStation 100
source control strategy 132, 133
SQL Administrator 154
SQL Server
licenses 56
SQL Server Reporting Services (SSRS) 131

SSO 89
stability 200
strategy 11, 12
Strengths, Weaknesses, Opportunities, and
    Threat. *See* SWOT analysis
Subject Matter Expert (SME) 181
Subversion (SVN) 133
Swiss Army knife 36
SWOT analysis 16
System Administrator 154
System Center Data Protection Manager
    2010 56
System Center Operations Manager 68
System Center Suite 84

T

Tableau Software 111
tablets 66
Team Foundation Server (TFS) 132, 133
TechCrunch
  URL 122
technology steering committee
  about 33
  alignment 33
  ownership 33
third-party hosting
  advantages 50
  drawbacks 50
Tibco Software 111
TopSharePoint
  about 102
  URL 102
training resources, SharePoint 156-158
Transparent Data Encryption (TDE) 92
treatment plan 17-19

U

UAT environment
  about 134
  building 134, 135
User Acceptance Testing environment. *See*
  UAT environment
user acceptance testing (UAT) 57
user-based CAL (User CAL) 53, 55
user-experience trends 101-104

V

VirtualBox 142
Virus checking 161
Visio 2010 130
Visio services 45, 47
Visual Source Safe (VSS) 132
Visual Studio 2010 129
Visual Studio Premium 152
Visual Studio Ultimate 152
VMW 142
VMWare 84, 142
Volkswagen Beetle 100
VPN 62

W

web browsers
  about 65
  levels 65
Web Content Accessibility Guidelines
    (WCAG) 105
web parts 128
Web Solution Packages (WSP) 128, 141
wikis 31
Windows Azure 75, 89, 96
Windows Azure, and SharePoint 2010
  data 90
  services 90
Windows Azure Content Delivery Network
    90
Windows infrastructure 83
Windows Server
  licenses 56
Windows Server 2008 142, 143
Windows SharePoint Services v3 (WSSv3)
    44
Wired
  URL 122
Word Automation Services 45
Workflow Foundation (WF) 178
workflows 128
workshop agenda, SharePoint IT strategy
  diagnostics 15, 17
  outcomes 20, 21
  SharePoint implementation plan 19, 20
  treatment plan 17-19

Thank you for buying
Microsoft SharePoint for Business Executives: Q&A Handbook

About Packt Publishing

Packt, pronounced 'packed', published its first book "Mastering phpMyAdmin for Effective MySQL Management" in April 2004 and subsequently continued to specialize in publishing highly focused books on specific technologies and solutions.

Our books and publications share the experiences of your fellow IT professionals in adapting and customizing today's systems, applications, and frameworks. Our solution based books give you the knowledge and power to customize the software and technologies you're using to get the job done. Packt books are more specific and less general than the IT books you have seen in the past. Our unique business model allows us to bring you more focused information, giving you more of what you need to know, and less of what you don't.

Packt is a modern, yet unique publishing company, which focuses on producing quality, cutting-edge books for communities of developers, administrators, and newbies alike. For more information, please visit our website: www.packtpub.com.

About Packt Enterprise

In 2010, Packt launched two new brands, Packt Enterprise and Packt Open Source, in order to continue its focus on specialization. This book is part of the Packt Enterprise brand, home to books published on enterprise software – software created by major vendors, including (but not limited to) IBM, Microsoft and Oracle, often for use in other corporations. Its titles will offer information relevant to a range of users of this software, including administrators, developers, architects, and end users.

Writing for Packt

We welcome all inquiries from people who are interested in authoring. Book proposals should be sent to author@packtpub.com. If your book idea is still at an early stage and you would like to discuss it first before writing a formal book proposal, contact us; one of our commissioning editors will get in touch with you.

We're not just looking for published authors; if you have strong technical skills but no writing experience, our experienced editors can help you develop a writing career, or simply get some additional reward for your expertise.

Microsoft SharePoint 2010 End User Guide: Business Performance Enhancement

ISBN: 978-1-84968-066-0   Paperback: 424 pages

A from-the-trenches tutorial filled with hints, tips, and real world best practices for applying SharePoint 2010 to your business

1. Designed to offer applicable, no-coding solutions to dramatically enhance the performance of your business

2. Excel at SharePoint intranet functionality to have the most impact on you and your team

3. Drastically enhance your End user SharePoint functionality experience

Microsoft SharePoint 2010 Power User Cookbook

ISBN: 978-1-84968-288-6   Paperback: 344 pages

Over 70 advanced recipes for expert End Users to unlock and apply the value of SharePoint

1. Discover how to apply SharePoint far beyond basic functionality

2. Explore the Business Intelligence capabilities of SharePoint with KPIs and custom dashboards

3. Take a deep dive into document management, data integration, electronic forms, and workflow scenarios

Please check **www.PacktPub.com** for information on our titles